Through the legislation maze series

This guide is the first in a new series, *Through the legislation maze,* which is intended to comprise short, easy to use, topic based guides to legislation, for construction professionals (architects, engineers, surveyors, facilities managers, contractors) and students in construction related fields. It will focus on aspects of design and job management that are controlled by several statutory instruments and related codes and approved documents, and where, in practice, assimilating these can be difficult and time consuming.

The series will provide 'maps' to guide readers round the various relevant publications, with explanatory discussion as to their significance and relevance. It will indicate which documents (and sections of documents) should be consulted in any given design context (for example, relating to building type, use, location, etc), and which are particularly relevant at each RIBA Work Stage. It will also cover commonly occurring problems and give lists of 'watch points' (highlighted in the text by ❶) relating to the topic. As the primary purpose is to 'point people in the right direction', the series will contain only limited discussion of the technical content of the legislation, but will refer the reader to other technical texts for detailed commentary.

Intended future topics in the series are:

The building logbook
Health and safety
Fire safety
Inclusive design
Structure and construction
The building envelope
Vertical circulation
Damp-proofing
Mixed use development

The series will provide a quick reference point for use during a working project, set out on a work stage basis. It will provide practical, management based guides, pointing out the operational implications of the legislation (for example, when other consultants may need to be brought in), cross linking the subject to different pieces of legislation and assessing the combined effect on aspects of design and job management. It will expand on issues pinpointed in the *Architect's Job Book* and the *Green Guide to the Architect's Job Book,* and provide a bridge between these and existing technical publications.

Through the legislation maze: energy conservation

The first guide in the series looks at energy conservation. In some ways this is an atypical topic, as the majority of the legislation relating to energy conservation in the design of buildings is to be found under one key statutory instrument, the Building Regulations 2000 Part L (Conservation of Fuel and Power) (as amended). However guidance to Part L is found in the Approved Documents L1 (dwellings) and L2 (buildings other than dwellings), which in turn refer to a wide variety of other documents, such as BRE and CIBSE publications.

Like Part L certain sections of Part H (Drainage and Waste Disposal) and Part J (Combustion Appliances and Fuel Storage Systems) are also concerned with environmental aspects of design, rather than health and safety, and in a broad but peripheral sense relate to energy conversation. In practical terms these Parts of the Building Regulations may need to be considered at the same time as provision is made for meeting the requirements of Part L and for that reason brief notes about these have been included in this guide.

The guide gives a general overview of the subject. It then goes on to outline the statutory framework and to highlight the recent changes resulting from the new Parts L1, L2, and relevant sections of Parts H and J. It then goes through each Work Stage highlighting which particular aspects may need to be considered at each stage. A list of references and further reading is given at the end of each section.

The authors would like to thank Professor Phil Jones and Robert Cooper of the Welsh School of Architecture for their helpful comments on the draft of this text.

Contents

1.	Background to the new provisions	1
2.	Overview of the legislation	3
	The statutory framework	3
	The key requirements and means of compliance: Part L	4
	Key changes to Parts L1 and L2	5
	Part L1 (dwellings)	5
	Part L2 (buildings other than dwellings)	5
	Other changes to the Regulations	5
	Key changes to the Approved Documents L1 and L2	6
	General changes to both ADL1 and ADL2	6
	Changes in ADL1 (dwellings) only	6
	Changes in ADL2 (buildings other than dwellings) only	7
	Key relevant changes to Parts H and J	7
	Part H: Drainage and Waste Disposal	7
	Part J: Combustion Appliances and Fuel Storage Systems	8
	Further information	8
3.	Application of the Regulations	9
	To what projects do the Regulations apply?	9
	When do they apply?	10
	To whom do they apply?	11
	References and further reading	11
4.	Work Stages: Pre-Agreement, A and B	13
	Pre-Agreement, Appraisal and Strategic Brief	13
	Application of the Regulations	15
	Part L	15
	Parts H and J	19
	References and further reading	20
5.	Work Stages: C, D and E	21
	Outline Proposals, Detail Proposals and Final Proposals	21
	Part L1 (dwellings)	21
	Elemental method (dwellings)	21
	Target U-value method (dwellings)	23
	Carbon Index method (dwellings)	23
	Part L2 (buildings other than dwellings)	25
	Elemental method (buildings other than dwellings)	25
	Whole-building method (buildings other than dwellings)	29
	Carbon emissions calculation method (buildings other than dwellings)	29
	References and further reading	31
6.	Work Stages: F, G and H	33
	Production Information, Tender Documents and Tender Action	33
	Continuity of insulation	33
	Air leakage tests	34
	Commissioning of systems	34
	Local Authority tests	34

Contents

	References and further reading	36
7.	Work Stages: J, K and L	37
	Mobilisation, Practical Completion and After	37
	Operating and Maintenance instructions for building services	37
	Notices	38
	Energy rating of dwellings	38
	SAP 2001	38
	Energy rating notices	38
	Wastewater system notices	39
	References and further reading	39
8.	Appendices	41
	A. Approved Document L1: summary guide to use of this document	41
	B. Approved Document L2: summary guide to use of this document	44

1. Background to the new provisions

In recent years there has been a general shift by governments and policy makers away from the narrow aim of conservation of stock resources, such as oil, natural gas, coal, etc., to broader environmental aims which include the safeguarding of flow resources, such as water and air. For example, under the Kyoto Protocol, the UK is obligated to reduce, by the year 2012, its greenhouse gas emissions, including CO_2 emissions, to 12.5 per cent below 1990 levels. Buildings in total account for 46 per cent of the UK's CO_2 emissions or approximately 63.5 million tonnes of carbon per year. Dwellings alone account for 30 per cent of UK energy consumption and 28 per cent of the resulting CO_2 emissions. This policy shift is reflected in many of the recent changes to legislation which focus on ways of reducing the pollution of such natural resources.

Part L of the Building Regulations 2000, together with the latest amendments to be brought in through the Building (Amendment) Regulations 2001, is therefore concerned not so much with simply reducing energy use but is primarily aimed at reducing carbon emissions into the atmosphere. The new Part L amends the existing requirements by separating the requirements which apply to dwellings and to other buildings. It adds new requirements relating to lighting systems, solar overheating, mechanical ventilation systems, airtightness of the envelope and for the provision of information on services.

Energy use from appropriate renewable sources such as daylight, passive cooling, solar gain, etc., is now being recognised within the methodologies used in the Approved Documents (AD) L1 (dwellings) and L2 (buildings other than dwellings) as having a positive effect. Conversely, energy use that emits carbon dioxide into the polluted atmosphere is recognised as having a negative effect. So, for example, if electric heating (from grid electricity) is to be used as the sole source of space and water heating then under these latest amendments to the regulations there will be a need to have higher standards of thermal insulation in the building in order to compensate for the electricity's high carbon content. The current regulations increase the requirements on work to existing buildings, reflecting the awareness that carbon emissions need to be significantly reduced not only from new buildings but also from the existing building stock. Taken together, these changes will have an effect on the orientation, siting, design, construction, commissioning and operation of new buildings, including dwellings and other buildings, and on the nature of alterations to existing buildings.

In parallel with the recent changes to Part L, changes have been introduced to certain sections of Parts H and J, again through the Building (Amendment) Regulations 2001. Like the changes to Part L these are also concerned with environmental aspects of design. The relevant changes to Part H (Drainage and Waste Disposal) include new requirements to consult local authorities on recycling of waste, on building over sewers and separate systems of sewers and for the provision of information on wastewater treatment systems. Similarly, the latest amendments to Part J (Combustion Appliances and Fuel Storage Systems) include requirements aimed at protecting against oil pollution of boreholes, water and drainage courses, including the provision of information.

2. Overview of the legislation

The statutory framework

The principal and consolidating statute is the Building Act 1984. It empowers the Secretary of State to make regulations with respect to design and construction of buildings and the provision of services, fittings and equipment in or in connection with buildings for the following purposes:
- to secure health, safety and welfare and convenience of persons in or about buildings and of others who may be affected by buildings or matters connected with buildings;
- to conserve fuel and power; and
- to prevent waste, undue consumption, misuse or contamination of water.

In addition the Act covers the exemption of particular classes of buildings, the passing of plans, the determination of questions, tests for conformity with building regulations, breaches of building regulations, 'approved inspectors', and the duties and powers of local authorities in respect of the Act, including payment of compensation.

The making of building regulations is empowered under Section 1 of the Building Act. The current regulations are the Building Regulations 2000 as amended by the Building (Amendment) Regulations 2001 and the Building (Amendment) Regulations 2002.

❶ **The amendments introduced by the Building (Amendment) Regulations 2001 and 2002 are significant and the Regulations and the Amendments Regulations should always be read alongside each other.**

The Regulations apply to England (including Inner London) and Wales. The technical requirements under the Building Regulations are set out in Schedule 1. In accordance with Regulation 8 of the Building Regulations, the requirements in Parts A to K and N (with the exceptions of paragraphs H2 and J6) of Schedule 1 are limited to securing reasonable standards of health and safety for people in or about buildings (and any others who may be affected by buildings or matters connected with buildings). Paragraphs H2, J6, L and M are excluded from Regulation 8, H2 and J6 because they deal directly with the prevention of the contamination of water, Part L (Parts L1 and L2) because it deals with the conservation of fuel and power, and Part M because it deals with access and facilities for disabled people.

The requirements in Schedule 1 to the Building Regulations are stated in broad terms, and guidance as to what might satisfy these are given in the 'Approved Documents', which are provided for under the Building Act. In the front of the Approved Documents under 'Use of Guidance' it states:

> Approved Documents are intended to provide guidance for some of the more common building situations. However there may well be alternative ways of achieving compliance with the requirements. Thus there is no obligation to adopt any particular solution contained in an Approved Document if you prefer to meet the relevant requirement in some other way.

In spite of this assurance it should be noted that under the Building Act 1984 S.7 failure to follow the advice in an Approved Document may be relied upon in court proceedings (civil or criminal) as 'tending to establish liability' for breach of the Building Regulations.

❶ **Given the complex technical nature of the methods of demonstrating compliance now set out in Approved Document L1 and L2, attempting to meet the relevant requirements 'in some other way' could prove a difficult, lengthy and expensive option.**

The Approved Documents are published separately, and are extended and revised from time to time. The most relevant to this guide are Approved Documents L1, L2, and limited parts of H and J.

Overview of the legislation

The key requirements and means of compliance: Part L

The key requirements for conservation of fuel and power are set out in Schedule 1 to the Building (Amendment) Regulations 2001. Part L under the Schedule is subdivided into Part L1, covering dwellings, and Part L2, covering other types of buildings. The Building Regulations Schedule 1 requirements are:

Dwellings L1

Reasonable provision shall be made for the conservation of fuel and power in dwellings by:

(a) limiting the heat loss:
   (i) through the fabric of the building;
   (ii) from hot water pipes and hot air ducts used for space heating;
   (iii) from hot water vessels;
(b) providing space heating and hot water systems which are energy efficient;
(c) providing lighting systems with appropriate lamps and sufficient controls so that energy can be used efficiently (the requirement for sufficient controls in paragraph L1(c) applies only to external lighting systems fixed to the building);
(d) providing sufficient information with the heating and hot water services so that building occupiers can operate and maintain the services in such a manner as to use no more energy than is reasonable in the circumstances.

Buildings other than dwellings L2

Reasonable provision shall be made for the conservation of fuel and power in buildings other than dwellings by:

(a) limiting the heat losses and gains through the fabric of the building;
(b) limiting the heat loss:
   (i) from hot water pipes and hot air ducts used for space heating;
   (ii) from hot water vessels and hot water service pipes;
(c) providing space heating and hot water systems which are energy efficient;
(d) limiting exposure to solar overheating;
(e) making provision where air conditioning and mechanical ventilation systems are installed, so that no more energy needs to be used than is reasonable in the circumstances;
(f) limiting the heat gains by chilled water and refrigerant vessels and pipes and air ducts that serve air conditioning systems (requirements L2(e) and (f) apply only within buildings and parts of buildings where more than 200 m^2 of floor area is to be served by air conditioning or mechanical ventilation systems);
(g) providing lighting systems which are energy efficient (applies only within buildings and parts of buildings where more than 100 m^2 of floor area is to be served by artificial lighting);
(h) providing sufficient information with the relevant services so that the building can be operated and maintained in such a manner as to use no more energy than is reasonable in the circumstances.

The Approved Documents L1 and L2 set out means of achieving compliance with the regulations. These can be summarised as follows:

For dwellings the requirements would be met if:
- there are reasonable provisions for limiting heat loss through the building fabric (with the benefits of solar gain and more efficient heating systems being taken into account where appropriate). ADL1 gives three alternative methods which could be used to demonstrate reasonable provision for limiting heat loss through the building fabric:
   (i) Elemental method;
   (ii) Target U-value method; and
   (iii) Carbon Index method.
- the building is reasonably airtight;
- there are no significant thermal bridges in the building fabric;
- there are reasonable provisions for limiting heat loss from the mechanical installation including if:
   (i) pipework, ductwork and hot water vessels are insulated;
   (ii) the mechanical systems are reasonably energy efficient;
   (iii) there are controls in place to ensure that the mechanical systems are energy efficient;
   (iv) the lighting system is reasonably energy efficient;

(v) there are controls in place to ensure that the lighting systems are energy efficient;
(vi) the services in operation have been inspected and commissioned; and
(vii) there is information which would enable the end user to run the services in an energy efficient way.

For buildings other than dwellings the requirements would be met if:
- there are reasonable provisions for the conservation of fuel and power. ADL2 gives the following three alternative methods which could be used to demonstrate that reasonable provision has been made:
  (i) Elemental method;
  (ii) Whole-building method; and
  (iii) Carbon emissions calculation method.
- the services in operation have been inspected and commissioned; and
- there is information which would enable the end user to run the services in an energy efficient way. Some of this information is to be provided in the form of a 'building log'.

For buildings other than dwellings, many of the additional requirements listed above for dwellings (for example airtightness, the insulation of pipework and lighting) are absorbed into the three methods of demonstrating that reasonable provision for energy conservation has been made.

The above methods of meeting the Regulations' requirements are discussed in the next chapter.

Key changes to Parts L1 and L2

The key changes are contained in Schedule 1 to the Regulations. Part L of Schedule 1 which contains the technical requirements is now divided into Part L1 dealing with dwellings and Part L2 dealing with other buildings. New editions of Approved Documents L1 and L2 give guidance on ways of meeting these requirements.

The key changes to the regulations are as follows:

Part L1 (dwellings)
The requirement applying to heating and hot water systems has been changed to include overall system performance rather than just controls. This means that the boiler's seasonal efficiency, inspection and commissioning are now covered. New requirements are introduced covering:
- efficient internal and external lighting systems fixed to the dwelling;
- appropriate lamps and controls for external lighting; and
- provision of information for the end user so that they can operate and maintain the heating, hot water and external lighting systems in an energy efficient way.

Part L2 (buildings other than dwellings)
Within the existing requirement to limit heat transfer through the building fabric the effects of heat gains as well as heat losses are now included.

The requirement applying to heating and hot water systems has been changed to include overall system performance rather than just controls. This means that the boiler's seasonal efficiency, inspection and commissioning are now covered.

The requirement applying to lighting has been re-worded to require the provision of lighting systems which are energy efficient in buildings or parts of buildings where over 100 m^2 is to be served by artificial lighting. This would encompass luminaires in some types of buildings as well as lamp performance.

New requirements are introduced that cover:
- limiting a building's exposure to solar overheating;
- the efficiency of air conditioned and mechanically ventilated buildings – this requirement covers inspection and commissioning but is limited to apply to buildings having more than 200 m^2 of conditioned floor area;
- limiting the heat gains due to the operation of the mechanical system itself;
- providing information so that the end user can operate and maintain the service installation in an energy efficient way.

Other changes to the Regulations
Regulation 2: The definition of 'controlled service or fitting' has been expanded to include services and fittings in relation to which Part L (as well as Parts G, H and J) imposes a requirement. This means, for example, that certain work to air conditioning and mechanical ventilation systems will now constitute 'building work'.

Overview of the legislation

Regulation 3(1) however includes a new paragraph 3(1)(a) which limits the effect of the amendment of the definition of 'controlled service or fitting' so that, in relation to existing dwellings only, the provision (including replacement) of windows, glazed doors, boilers and hot water vessels is 'building work' but the provision of other 'Part L' controlled services is not. For existing buildings other than dwellings, provision (including replacement) of windows, exterior doors, boilers, hot water vessels, heating, ventilation, air conditioning and lighting is 'building work'.

❶ Due to the above two changes the provision, (including replacement), or extension, in existing as well as in new buildings, of services and fittings covered by Part L becomes regulated building work under Regulation 3(1)(b).

Regulation 12(5) has been replaced under the Buildings (Amendments) Regulations 2002. Exemptions from the requirement to give notice/deposit plans are extended to include a range of registered or approved persons carrying specified work to services, as set out on schedule 2A to the Regulations.

Regulation 16 of the Building Regulations continues to require that all new dwellings must be given an energy rating using the Standard Assessment Procedure (SAP) and the rating displayed as a notice. SAP 1988 has been superseded by SAP 2001, the final version of which was published in 2002. Changes in the Standard Assessment Procedure (SAP 2001) are as follows:
- the Carbon Index is introduced;
- the upper limit of the SAP rating is raised from 100 to 120;
- the SAP indexing function has been made less dependent on floor area;
- U-values are now based on European Standards;
- additional heating systems have been included; and
- data tables have been updated.

A new Regulation 16A has been introduced by the Building (Amendment) Regulations 2002. It provides that where building work which consists only of the replacement of a window, roof light, roof window or door is carried out by a person registered under the Fenestration Self Assessment Scheme, the Local Authority may accept a certificate by that person as evidence that the work complies with Regulations 6 and 7.

Regulation 18 granting local authorities powers to test work is amended to allow tests for compliance with all applicable provisions of Schedule 1, Part L.

Key changes to the Approved Documents L1 and L2

General changes to both ADL1 and ADL2
Under both Approved Documents thermal transmittance of building fabric elements (U-values) are now calculated by methods set out in the European Standards. New lower (improved) U-values have been set - for example, the nominal average U-values of windows and other glazed elements is now based on sealed double glazing units with 16 mm air gap and low emissivity inner pane.

Both Approved Documents indicate in places that a suitable approach to achieving and demonstrating the required performance can be by certification of compliance of a competent person or firm.

Both Approved Documents give more guidance on work in existing buildings including historic buildings.

Changes in ADL1 (dwellings) only
The Elemental method may now only be applied where high efficiency heating systems are to be used. There is little opportunity for design flexibility for new dwellings (for example, glazing area is restricted to not more than 25 per cent of floor area) but there are arrangements for trade-offs between fabric elements in alteration and extension work.

The Target U-Value method is retained and the provisions for trading off between fabric and heating system performance have been improved.

The Carbon Index method replaces the Energy Rating method which used Standard Assessment Procedure (SAP) ratings. SAP ratings must still be provided however to meet the requirements in Regulation 16 which call for SAP ratings to be notified to building control bodies and posted as notices in new dwellings whenever they are created either through new-build or as a result of a material change of use.

The guidance on reducing thermal bridging has been improved and new guidance is given on reducing unwanted air leakage.

There are new requirements for commissioning heating and hot water systems, for lighting and the provision of information.

Changes in ADL2 (buildings other than dwellings) only

The Elemental method now encompasses all aspects of showing compliance, not just the fabric thermal performance, and includes airtightness, the impact of solar gain on cooling load, and the efficiencies of the heating, ventilation, cooling and lighting systems. The guidance on reducing thermal bridging has been improved and new guidance is given on reducing unwanted air leakage. For air conditioning and mechanical ventilation systems in offices, a new Carbon Performance Rating method can be used to show compliance. Outside the office sector there is a simpler requirement for the efficiency of ventilation systems, measured as the 'Specific Fan Power'.

The Calculation and Energy Use methods have been replaced by the Whole-building method (with a carbon rating system for offices and carbon accounting methods for other types of buildings) and the Carbon Emissions Calculation method, which is based on the calculated annual carbon emissions of a 'notional building'.

New guidance is given on the requirement to establish that thermal resistance and airtightness standards have been achieved. Certification is required regarding continuity of insulation and airtightness, with the latter requiring an air leakage test for buildings over 1000 m^2.

Guidance is given on complying with the new requirements for avoiding solar overheating, on lighting fittings in offices and storage buildings, display lighting, air conditioning and mechanical ventilation and their testing, commissioning and certification.

Guidance is also given on the provision of information, including the provision of energy meters and building logbooks.

Key relevant changes to Parts H and J

Part H: Drainage and Waste Disposal

Section H1 of Schedule 1 to the Regulations now includes a general requirement of drainage. (This was originally the subject of Section 21 of the Building Act 1984.) The acceptable methods of discharge are specified in order of priority.

Adequate Notice

Under a new requirement H(2)(3), where a foul water drainage system from a building discharges to a septic tank, wastewater treatment system or cesspool, a durable notice is now required to be posted in a suitable place in the building, containing information on any continuing maintenance required to avoid risks to health.

Contaminated run-offs

Section H3 of Schedule 1 has been expanded and now includes a general requirement of rainwater drainage. The acceptable methods of discharge are specified in order of priority. Under new requirements H5 any rainwater discharge to a sewer must be separate from any system provided to discharge foul water to that sewer. Approved Document H3 paragraph 3.21, deals with drainage from areas where materials are stored which could contaminate runoff. This could cause pollution if discharged to a surface water sewer. Where such flows are to be discharged into the foul sewer system, the consent of the sewerage undertaker should first be obtained in accordance with Section 106 (Right to communicate with public sewers) of the Water Industry Act 1991. The sewerage undertaker should also be consulted where such flows are to be discharged into a foul drain which, though it would initially connect to a combined sewer, it is intended that this would eventually be reconnected to a proposed foul sewer.

Overview of the legislation

Building over sewers
A new section H4 has been introduced which requires that where erecting, extending or underpinning a building over sewers, the work should be carried out in such a way as to be detrimental to the building, extending or maintenance of the sewer. These situations were previously dealt with under Section 18 of the Building Act, which has been repeated with effect from 1 April 2002.

Recycling of waste
Section H6 has been expanded. The waste collection authority has powers under Section 46 (Receptacles for household waste) and Section 47 (Receptacles for commercial or industrial waste) of the Environmental Protection Act 1990 to specify the type and number of receptacles to be used and the location where the waste should be placed for collection. Adequate means of access should be provided from the place of storage to a collection point. Consultation should take place with the waste collection authority to determine their requirements.

For domestic developments space should be provided for storage of containers for separated waste (i.e. waste which can be recycled is stored separately from waste which cannot) having a combined capacity of 0.25 m^2 per dwelling or such other capacity as may be agreed with the waste collection authority.

For non domestic developments, the local waste collection authority should be consulted for guidance on dealing with their requirements for segregation of waste which can be recycled.

Part J: Combustion Appliances and Fuel Storage Systems

Adequate Notice
A new requirement J4 calls for a notice providing the performance characteristics of the hearth, fireplace, flue or chimney to be fixed in an appropriate place.

Safety aspect
A new requirement J5 calls for oil and liquid petroleum gas fuel storage systems to be positioned and/or shielded so as to protect them from fires that could occur in adjacent buildings or on adjacent property.

Pollution
A new requirement J6 makes provisions for protection against oil pollution of boreholes, water and drainage courses and for permanent labels containing information on how to respond to oil escapes to be positioned in a prominent position. New guidance is given on assessing the risk of pollution and the necessary, reasonable measures to contain leaks.

Further information

Building Regulations can be found on the HMSO website at www.hmso.gov.uk

The Building Regulations 2000 can be found at http://www.hmso.gov.uk/si/si2000/20002531.htm and the Building (Amendment) Regulations 2001 at http://www.hmso.gov.uk/si/si2001/20013335.htm

The Approved Documents can be found at http://www.safety.odpm.gov.uk/bregs/brads.htm

There is a useful site for 'Frequently Asked Questions' relating to Part L at http://projects.bre.co.uk/partlfaq/default.htm

www.bre.co.uk and www.bsria.co.uk both contain information on designing to meet the new regulations, lists of publications and seminar programmes.

3. Application of the Regulations

To what projects do the Regulations apply?

The application of the Building Regulations depends on the meaning of the terms 'building work' and 'material change of use' (i.e. Regulation 4 requires 'building work' to be carried out to comply with the requirements of Schedule 1, and Regulation 6 imposes certain requirements on work relating to a material change of use).

The definition of 'material change of use' remains as it is in the Building Regulations 2000 (see Figure 1). The definition of 'building work', however, has been expanded by the Building (Amendment) Regulations 2001, and is now as follows:

> 3. (1) In these Regulations 'building work' means:
>
>   (a) the erection or extension of a building;
>   (b) subject to paragraph (1A), the provision or extension of a controlled service or fitting in or in connection with a building;
>   (c) the material alteration of a building, or a controlled service or fitting, as mentioned in paragraph (2);
>   (d) work required by Regulation 6 (requirements relating to material change of use);
>   (e) the insertion of insulating material into the cavity wall of a building;
>   (f) work involving the underpinning of a building.
>
>   (1A) The provision or extension of a controlled service or fitting:
>
>   (a) in or in connection with an existing dwelling; and
>   (b) being a service or fitting in relation to which paragraph L1, but not Part G, H or J, of Schedule 1 imposes a requirement. Shall only be building work where that work consists of the provision of a window, roof light, roof window, door (being a door which together with its frame has more than 50 per cent of its internal face area glazed), a space heating or hot water service boiler, or a hot water vessel.
>
>   (2) An alteration is material for the purposes of these Regulations if the work, or any part of it, would at any stage result:
>
>   (a) in a building or controlled service or fitting not complying with a relevant requirement where previously it did; or
>   (b) in a building or controlled service or fitting which before the work commenced did not comply with a relevant requirement, being more unsatisfactory in relation to such a requirement.
>
>   (3) In paragraph (2) 'relevant requirements' means any of the following applicable requirements:
>   Part A (structure);
>   Paragraph B1 (means of warning and escape);
>   Paragraph B3 (internal fire spread – structure);
>   Paragraph B4 (external fire spread);
>   Paragraph B5 (access and facilities for the fire service);
>   Paragraph M (access and facilities for disabled people).

The effect of 1A is that under 3(i)(b) the provision or extension of a controlled service or fitting in relation to an existing dwelling where L1 (but not G or H) imposes a requirement on such services/fittings is only 'building work' where it is the type of work listed under 1A.

❗ Under 3(i)(c) Part L is not a 'relevant requirement' for the purposes of defining 'material alteration', but that once work falls under the definition of 'material alteration' Part L may be an applicable requirement.

In summary, the requirements of Part L of the Building Regulations now apply to: the erection or extension or material alteration of new dwellings, and new 'other buildings'; the provision, extension or material alteration of controlled services or fittings (as qualified by Regulation 3(1A)); and work in connection with a material change of use.

Application of the regulations

Figure 1: Meaning of material change of use (Building Regulations 2000)

> Regulation 5. For the purposes of paragraph 8(1)(e) of Schedule 1 to the Act and for the purposes of these Regulations, there is a material change of use where there is a change in the purposes for which or the circumstances in which a building is used, so that after that change:
>
> (a) the building is used as a dwelling, where previously it was not;
>
> (b) the building contains a flat, where previously it did not;
>
> (c) the building is used as an hotel or a boarding house, where previously it was not;
>
> (d) the building is used as an institution, where previously it was not;
>
> (e) the building is used as a public building, where previously it was not;
>
> (f) the building is not a building described in Classes I to VI in Schedule 2, where previously it was; or
>
> (g) the building, which contains at least one dwelling, contains a greater or lesser number of dwellings than it did previously.

When do they apply?

The Building Regulations 2000 took effect on 1 January 2001. The Building (Amendment) Regulations 2001 came into force on 1 April 2002. Transitional Provisions for Part L are set out in DTLR Circular 03/2001 Annex E.

The changes do not apply in relation to building work which has started before 1 April 2002, provided that such work began in accordance with:
- a building notice and a commencement notice given to the local authority; or
- full plans deposited with and a commencement notice given to the local authority; or
- an initial notice, an amendment notice or a public body's notice given to the local authority.

The changes do not apply in relation to building work which has started on or after 1 April 2002 where:
- full plans were deposited before 1 April 2002 and the local authority has passed the plans without conditions before that date; or
- full plans were deposited before 1 April 2002 and the local authority has stated in writing before that date, that any conditions subject to which they passed the plans have been fully met; or
- a plans certificate was given by an approved inspector to a local authority before that date and was accepted (or was deemed to have been accepted) before, on or after that date.

In cases which involve more than one building, such as a housing estate, then the changes apply to the buildings where was not started before 1 April 2002 unless such work fulfils the above conditions.

For buildings other than dwellings there is an interim period up to and including the 30 September 2003 in relation to what are the acceptable procedures used as a means of showing compliance with air tightness of construction.

Guidance on transitional arrangements for the use of the new edition of *The Standard Assessment Procedure* (SAP 2001) is given in *The Building Act and its Regulations*, a DTLR 'circular letter' of the 12 February 2002. The circular letter states that:

> ...between now and 30 June 2002, energy ratings may be calculated and notified to building control bodies, for the purposes of Regulations 16 and 12, using either SAP 1998 or SAP 2001. Energy ratings calculated for the purposes of Regulations 16 and 12, notified to building control bodies on or after 1 July 2002, must be calculated using SAP 2001. Where an energy rating has been calculated using SAP 1998 and notified to the building control body before 1 July 2002, but on

that date a notice of the rating has not yet been posted up in the dwelling (or given to the occupier) pursuant to Regulation 16 or Regulation 12, the posted-up notice (or notice given to the occupier) must give the SAP 1998 rating. It would, however, be open to builders in these circumstances to provide a SAP 2001 rating in addition to the SAP 1998 rating.

❗ The final version of SAP 2001 was published in early 2002, and included corrections to the earlier 2001 edition, which were issued in the form of an 'errata' supplement.

To whom do they apply?

It is a general characteristic of the Building Acts and Regulations that they do not make it precisely clear who owes the duty imposed, i.e. whether it is owner, occupier, consultant, contractor or sub-contractor.

The format of the majority of regulations is to impose the requirement on the work that is carried out, for example under Regulation 4 of the Building Regulations which states:

Building work must be carried out so that … it complies with the regulations applicable requirements.

In practical terms, as it is the client who may ultimately be subject to an enforcement notice should the works be found not to comply, then it is in the client's interests to ensure that the specific duties are clearly allocated amongst those who are engaged to carry out the building project.

At other points in the Regulations duties are ascribed to particular persons, for example prior to work being carried out:

A person who intends to carry out building work shall give notice or deposit full plans (Reg. 12)

A person who proposes to carry out building work shall not commence that work unless… he has given local authority notice (Reg. 15)

and, while work is underway:

A person carrying out building work shall not… cover up any excavation unless he has given notice (Reg. 15)

and on completion:

The person carrying out the building work shall calculate the energy rating of the dwelling (Reg. 16)

It is generally considered that 'a person' as referred to above is not limited to the person who physically carries out the building work but includes also the owner of the premises on which the work is to be carried out and who authorises the works.

In all cases, if the owner or client wishes to ensure that these duties are carried by a specific party then their contract with that party will have to reflect that requirement.

❗ The Approved Document may appear to be assuming, at certain points, that a given party will be carrying out a certain activity, but this should be treated with caution. For example where, in the 'summary guide', it states 'Additional checks to be carried out by builders' it is again not necessarily referring solely to the person who is physically carrying out the work, but is using 'builder' in the wider sense described above. If it is intended that the contractor and/or sub-contractor is to be responsible for a specific aspect then this should be made clear in the contract documents.

References and further reading

BRESCU, 2002: *The Government's Standard Assessment Procedure for Energy Rating of Dwellings,* Garston, Watford.

DTLR Circular 03/2001 Annex E.

The Building Act and its Regulations, a DTLR 'circular letter' of the 12 February 2002.

4. Work Stages: Pre-Agreement, A and B

Pre-Agreement
Appraisal
Strategic Brief

One of the most notable implications of the recent changes to Part L, as well as to the relevant sections of Parts H and J, is that it is now essential to give early consideration to a number of design issues that might previously have been left to a later work stage.

At Pre-Agreement stage a potential client will need to be informed of any particular requirements in relation to the appointment of technical consultants. At the Appraisal and Strategic Brief stages, the effect of the regulations will need to be taken into account when considering the feasibility of the project.

In particular the effects of the regulations will need to be examined in order to establish whether they will require:
- earlier input by technical consultants;
- an increase in the input by technical consultants;
- an increase in the cost of the usable building; and
- an increase in the costs associated with testing, commissioning and certification.

Some of the recent changes may require earlier consultations with statutory authorities and earlier and more extensive input from technical consultants. For example, the method selected to demonstrate compliance with Part L1 or L2 will affect the degree of flexibility possible in the design and technical detailing of the project. If an innovative design is contemplated, this will require the use of a more complex method of demonstration, which will in turn require more extensive input from specialist technical consultants, who may need to be brought in to the design team right at the start of the project (see Table 1).

❗ **The client must be advised of the need for these early consultations and specialist input, and that resources will need to be allocated for this.**

The revised requirements for lower U-values for elements of the building, the revised requirements for insulation of pipes and ducts and the requirements for efficient mechanical ventilation (in the case of L2), may have a noticeable effect on the building costs, as well as an increase in the ratio of gross to net floor areas. The combination of these factors will have the effect of increasing the cost of the usable area of the building.

Allowance should also be made for increased project costs due to the new requirements for testing and commissioning of systems, certifying that the system as provided meets the regulations, and the provision of notices and information to the occupiers.

❗ **The client must be advised of these possible increases in project costs, and these must be fully accounted for in the preparation of any feasibility study.**

It is therefore important at this early stage to determine whether all or some of the requirements of Part L1 or Part L2 would apply to a particular project, as this will affect its feasibility. The extent of application of the new regulations is affected by various characteristics of the project. Those that are particularly relevant to Work Stages A and B (building use, whether new-build or alterations to existing, whether the project is a historic building, site characteristics) are dealt with below whereas those relating to Work Stages C to E (floor area of building/extension, orientation of building) are dealt with in the next chapter (see Table 2).

Work Stages: Pre-Agreement, A and B

Table 1 Specialist input and consultations

Project characteristic	Input/consultations	Applicable regulations	Covered in Chapter
Degree of design flexibility needed, (will determine method used to demonstrate compliance with Part L)	Early input from building services engineers	Part L1 or Part L2	5
Orientation, siting, extent and configuration of glazing (for example, in the case of dwellings, if advantage is to be taken of potential trade-offs in relation to solar gains)	Early input from planning consultant/early consultation with planning authority	Part L1 or Part L2	5
Artificial ventilation/air conditioning strategy, (for example, low velocity systems will require larger service ducts which in turn may affect structural dimensions and usable floor areas)	Early input from building services engineers	Part L2	5
Historic buildings, (some conservation areas may have policies that contain restrictions which conflict with Part L)	Early consultations with the local authority conservation officers and Building Control	Part L1 or Part L2	4
Disposal of wastewater	Early consultations with the Environment Agency	Part H2	4
Disposal of rainwater	Survey of the site and adjoining water courses	Part H3	4
Siting of building in relation to sewers	Survey of the site and of the neighbouring land	Part H4	4
Collection of waste – siting of containers	Early consultations with waste collection authorities	Part H6	4
Provision of containers for separate waste for recycling	Early consultations with waste collection authorities	Part H6	4
Siting of fuel storage systems in relation to adjacent buildings	Survey of the site and of the neighbouring land	Part J	4

Table 2 Sections of this guide covering specific project characteristics and applicable regulations

Project characteristic	Applicable regulations	Covered in Chapter
New building or substantial alterations to an existing building	Part L1 or Part L2	4
Building use – dwelling or building other than dwelling or as a mixed use building	Part L1 or Part L2	4, 5, 6 and 7
Total floor area of extension	Part L1 or Part L2	5
Total floor area of proposed building	Part L1 or Part L2	5

Application of the Regulations

PART L

Building use
For Part L of the regulations the requirements differ between dwellings and buildings other than dwellings. The requirements to show compliance for buildings other than dwellings will need more input from specialist consultants, and this input may be required earlier in the project.

Although the requirements of Part L2 (other buildings) are no less stringent than those of Part L1 (dwellings), the way of demonstrating compliance to Part L2 has been mainly internalised into each of the three alternative methods. This allows for greater design flexibility, but at the cost of greater specialist input.

❗ **The shared areas in mixed use buildings (dwellings and other buildings) are required to meet the requirements for other buildings, i.e. L2, where the requirements of L1 and L2 differ.**

New build or alterations to existing
Part L (L1 and L2) applies to all new buildings and also to certain work to existing buildings. Application to new building is dealt with in the next chapter. Where work is being carried out in connection with an existing building, whether or not it needs to comply will depend on whether the work is to a dwelling or other building, whether it constitutes a 'material alteration' or 'material change of use', or whether the work is to a 'controlled service or fitting'.

Table 3 sets out work that needs to comply with Part L1 and/or Part L2 in connection with Material Alterations and Material Change of Use to existing buildings and how the requirements can be met. (A detailed definition of Material Alteration is given in ADL1 paragraphs 2.4 and 2.5, and ADL2 paragraphs 4.5 and 4.6; and Material Change of Use is given in ADL1 paragraphs 2.7 and 2.8 and ADL2 paragraphs 4.8 and 4.9.)

Similarly, Tables 4 and 5 set out work that needs to comply with Part L1 and/or Part L2 in connection with work relating to controlled services and fittings in existing buildings.

Historic buildings
The Approved Documents give the following guidance in relation to historic buildings (ADL1 paragraph 2.10 and ADL2 paragraph 4.11):

> The aim should be to improve energy efficiency where and to the extent that it is practically possible, always provided that the work does not prejudice the character of the historic building, or increase the risk of long-term deterioration to the building fabric or fittings. In arriving at an appropriate balance between historic building conservation and energy conservation, it would be appropriate to take into account the advice of the local planning authority's conservation officer.

Such advice, which relates to all buildings, would cover issues such as:
- the restoration of a building's historic character, which may include the replacement windows, doors and roof lights;
- the rebuilding of a former historic building; and
- improving the longevity of a historic building by, for example, enabling the fabric of historic buildings to 'breathe'.

❗ **When working with historic buildings it will be essential to liaise at an early stage with the Local Authority Conservation Officer to establish whether there are any policies in relation to any parts of the building (e.g. windows) which might conflict with Part L. The extent of required compliance with Part L can then be discussed at an early stage with Building Control.**

Table 3 Existing buildings: Material Alterations and Material Change of Use: work that needs to comply with Part L1 and/or Part L2

Element	Regulations apply	L1 and/ or L2	Other Requirements to be met	Requirements met by	Regulations apply
Accessible lofts	When upgrading insulation where use is changed to that of a dwelling	Parts L1 and L2		Providing additional insulation to achieve a U-value not exceeding 0.25 W/m^{2}K where the existing insulation provides a U-value worse than 0.35 W/m^{2}K.	In connection with Material Change of Use only
Roof insulation	When substantially replacing any of the major elements of a roof structure	Parts L1 and L2		Providing insulation to achieve the U-value for new buildings	In connection with Material Alterations and/or Material Change of Use
Floor insulation	Where the structure of a ground floor is to be substantially replaced or reboarded	Parts L1 and L2		Providing insulation in heated rooms to the standard for new buildings	In connection with Material Alterations and/or Material Change of Use
Wall insulation	When substantially replacing complete exposed walls or their external renderings or cladding or internal surface finishes, or the internal surfaces of separating walls to unheated spaces	Parts L1 and L2		Providing a reasonable thickness of insulation	In connection with Material Alterations and/or Material Change of Use
Sealing measures	When carrying out any of the above work	Parts L1 and L2	Requirements of Parts F and J should be taken into account	Including reasonable sealing measures to improve airtightness	In connection with Material Alterations and/or Material Change of Use
Lighting	When providing lighting where use is changed to that of a dwelling	Part L1 only		Providing lighting in accordance with the guidance in paras. 1.54 to 1.57	In connection with Material Change of Use only
Controlled services and fittings	When replacing controlled services and fittings	Parts L1 and L2		See Tables 4 and 5 below	In connection with Material Alterations and/or Material Change of Use

Work Stages: Pre-Agreement, A and B

Table 4 Existing buildings: Work on controlled services or fittings:
work that needs to comply with Part L1 and (in most cases) Part L2

Services or fittings	Regulations apply	L1 and/or L2	Other requirements to be met	Requirements met by	Limits of requirements	Regulations do not apply
Windows, doors and roof lights	Wherever undertaking replacement work	Parts L1 and L2	The replacement work to comply with Parts L and N, and be no worse than applicable to Parts of Schedule 1, including Parts B, F and J	Average U-value not to exceed the appropriate entry in Table 1 of ADL1 and ADL2, or with a centre-pane U-value not exceeding 1.2 W/m^{2}K		Repair work on parts of these elements, such as replacing broken glass or sealed double-glazing units or replacing rotten framing members
Heating boilers	Wherever heating boilers are to be replaced in dwellings having a floor area greater than 50 m^2 and heating systems in buildings other than dwellings	Parts L1 and L2	For buildings other than dwellings requirements of Parts F and J should be taken into account	Providing a new boiler as if for a new dwelling or a new installation in buildings other than dwellings. Detailed guidance is given for dwellings in para. 2.3b of ADL1	In the case of replacement boilers installed in the period up to 31 August 2002, it would be reasonable to provide a less efficient boiler provided the heating controls comply with specification HR2 or HC2 given in GIL 59	
Hot water vessels	Wherever undertaking replacement work	Parts L1 and L2		Providing new equipment as if for a new dwelling. Detailed guidance is given in para. 1.43 of ADL1		
Boiler and hot water storage controls	See above	Parts L1 and L2		The work may also need to include replacement of the time switch or programmer, room thermostat, and hot water vessel thermostat, and provision of a boiler interlock and fully pumped circulation. For dwellings, detailed guidance is given in paras.1.23(d) and (e) of ADL1	In the case of dwellings other than solid fuel boilers	
Boiler and hot water storage	Where heating and hot water systems are to be altered as above	Part L	Commissioning and providing operating and maintenance instructions	Commissioning and providing operating and maintenance instructions. Detailed guidance is given in paras. 1.47 to 1.51 of ADL1		

Table 5 Existing buildings: Work on controlled services or fittings: work that needs to comply with Part L2 only

Services or fittings	Regulations apply	Requirements met by	Regulations do not apply
Lighting systems	When replacing a complete lighting system serving more than 100 m² of floor area	Providing a new lighting system as if for a new building i.e. ADL2 1.43 to 1.59	
Lighting systems	Where only the complete luminaires are being replaced	Providing new luminaires that meet the standards given in ADL2 paras. 1.43 or 1.48	Where only components such as lamps or louvres are being replaced
Lighting systems	Where only the control system is to be replaced	Providing new controls that meet the standards in ADL2 paras. 1.56 to 1.58	Where only components such as switches and relays are being replaced
Air conditioning or mechanical ventilation systems	When installing a complete acmv system to serve more than 200 m² of floor area in office buildings	Provide new ACMV system as if for new building (i.e. ADL2 paras 1.61 to 1.64)	
Air conditioning or mechanical ventilation systems	When extending an existing system to serve more than 200 m² of floor area in office buildings	Improving the Carbon Performance Rating in line with ADL2 para. 1.65	
Air conditioning or mechanical ventilation systems	Where substantial alterations are made to existing system serving more than 200 m² of floor area in office buildings	Improving the Carbon Performance Rating in line with ADL2 para. 1.65	
Air conditioning or mechanical ventilation systems	Where replacing existing equipment only, in system serving more than 200 m² of floor area in office buildings	Compliance with guidance in ADL2 para. 1.66	
Air conditioning or mechanical ventilation systems	When replacing air conditioning or mechanical ventilation systems in buildings other than offices or dwellings	Provide mechanical ventilation systems that meet the Specific Fan Power standards in ADL2 para. 1.67	
Heating, hot water, lighting and air conditioning or mechanical ventilation systems	When replacing air conditioning or mechanical ventilation systems in buildings other than dwellings	Inspect and commission the work; prepare and provide the building logbook or update as necessary; prepare a metering strategy or revise so as to enable the energy consumption of the replacement controlled service or fitting to be effectively monitored. Detailed guidance is given in ADL2 para. 4.4	

PARTS H and J

As discussed in the introduction, Parts H Drainage and Waste Disposal and J Combustion Appliances and Fuel Storage Systems now contain requirements that relate to environmental matters. These new requirements may be of particular interest during early work stages as they may influence the siting or configuration of a building.

❗ **Early consultations with statutory authorities and input from specialist consultants may be needed in relation to Parts H and J requirements.**

Part H: Foul water drainage

A general requirement of drainage is now included in Part H1 of Schedule 1 to the Regulations (originally the subject of Section 21 of the Building Act 1984):

> An adequate system of drainage shall be provided to carry foul water from appliances within the building to one of the following, listed in order of priority:
>
> (a) a public sewer; or, where that is not reasonably practicable,
> (b) a private sewer communicating with a public sewer; or, where that is not reasonably practicable,
> (c) either a septic tank which has an appropriate form of secondary treatment or another wastewater treatment system; or, where that is not reasonably practicable,
> (d) a cesspool.

A wastewater treatment system may be a septic tank, together with a drainage field or other means of secondary treatment, or other wastewater treatment system and must comply with requirements of Schedule H2. Note that the means of discharge are now given an order of priority. The approved document (only) gives guidance on the general principles relating to capacity, siting and ventilation of cesspools and wastewater treatment systems. Any discharge from a wastewater treatment system is likely to require a consent from the Environment Agency.

Initial contact with the Environment Agency is made as part of the planning procedures for non-mains drainage. Where there have not previously been such discussions with the Environment Agency, those seeking Building Regulations approval for non-mains drainage should contact the area office of the Environment Agency in order to determine whether a consent to discharge is required and what parameters apply. Further information is available in the Environment Agency's Pollution Prevention Guideline No 4: *Disposal of sewage where no mains drainage is available*.

Part H: Rainwater drainage

A general requirement of rainwater drainage is now included in Part H3, which refers to adequate provision for drainage of both roofs and paved areas around buildings. Paragraph H3(3) then states that rainwater drainage systems:

Shall discharge to one of the following, listed in order of priority:

(a) an adequate soakaway or some other adequate infiltration system; or, where that is not reasonably practicable
(b) a watercourse; or, where that is not reasonably practicable
(c) a sewer.

Part H: Building over sewers

A new requirement H4(1) states:

> The erection or extension of a building or work involving the underpinning of a building shall be carried out in a way that is not detrimental to the building or building extension or to the continued maintenance of the drain, sewer or disposal main.

This deals with situations previously covered by Section 18 of the Building Act 1984 (Section 18 is repealed, subject to transitional provisions, with effect from 1 April 2002).

Part H: Relevant waste collection legislation – Collection of household waste

Under Section 45 (Collection of controlled waste) of the Environmental Protection Act 1990, local authorities have a general duty to collect household waste within their area without charge. Under Section 46 (Receptacles for household waste) of the Environmental Protection Act 1990, the local authority still may require:

(a) waste of certain types to be stored separately so that it can be recycled;
(b) occupiers of dwellings to provide containers of a specified type for storage of waste;
(c) additional containers to be provided for separate storage of recyclable waste;
(d) locations where containers should be placed for emptying.

Part H: Relevant waste collection legislation – Collection of commercial and industrial waste

Under Section 45 (Collection of controlled waste) of the Environmental Protection Act 1990, local authorities may also have a duty to collect commercial waste within their area where requested and they may also collect industrial waste. A charge may be levied for such services. Under Section 47 (Receptacles for commercial or industrial waste) of the Environmental Protection Act 1990, the local authority may still require:

(a) waste of certain types to be stored separately so that it can be recycled;
(a) occupiers to provide containers of a specified type for storage of waste;
(c) additional containers to be provided for separate storage of recyclable waste;
(d) locations where containers should be placed for emptying.

Under revised requirement H6 of the Building Regulations adequate means of access must be provided from the place of storage to a collection point, where one has been specified by the waste collection authority under Section 46 (household waste) or Section 47 (commercial waste) of the Environmental Protection Act 1990(b) or to a street (where no collection point has been specified).

❗ **Careful consideration will need to be given to storage of waste and access to collection points at an early stage in the design of housing, commercial or industrial projects.**

Part J

New requirement J5 now calls for oil and liquid petroleum gas fuel storage systems to be positioned and/or shielded so as to protect them from fires that could occur in adjacent buildings or on adjacent property.

New requirement J6 makes provisions for protection against oil pollution of boreholes, water and drainage courses and for permanent labels containing information on how to respond to oil escapes to be located in a prominent position.

Guidance is given in the related Approved Document on assessing the risk of pollution and the necessary, reasonable measures to contain leaks for the components of prefabricated appliance chambers.

Part J applies to the accommodation of any combustion installation and liquid fuel storage system and Approved Document J has been prepared mainly with domestic installations in mind (see Section 0, paragraph 0.1). For installations with higher output ratings than those noted in the Approved Document, specialist guidance may be necessary. In certain cases larger installations may show compliance by adopting recommendations of CIBSE Design Guide Volume B and practice standard produced by BSI and the Institute of Gas Engineers.

❗ **Where oil and liquid petroleum gas fuel storage systems are to be used, careful consideration will need to be given to siting and prevention of pollution.**

References and further reading

CIBSE Design Guide Volume B: *Installation and equipment data*.

Environment Agency's Pollution Prevention Guideline No 4: *Disposal of sewage where no mains drainage is available*.

GIL 59, 2000: *Central heating system specifications (CheSS)*, BRESCU.

GPG 155, 2001: *Energy efficient refurbishment of existing housing*, BRESCU.

GPG 302, 2001: *Controls for domestic central heating and hot water*, BRESCU.

5. Work Stages: C, D and E

Outline Proposals
Detail Proposals
Final Proposals

During these work stages applications are submitted for Town and Country Planning approval and Building Regulation consent. It is therefore at this stage that it will be necessary to demonstrate compliance with the Regulations to the Local Authority.

The Approved Documents L1 and L2 each contain a step by step table which can be used to help determine the method of compliance most suited to a particular project. These are reproduced in this guide in Appendices A and B.

Part L1 (dwellings)

Limiting heat loss (dwellings)
Requirement L1(a) of Schedule 1 of the Regulations stipulates that dwellings should make reasonable provisions for limiting the heat loss:
- through the fabric of the building;
- from hot water pipes and hot air ducts used for space heating; and
- from hot water vessels.

The ADL1 gives three methods which could be used to demonstrate that reasonable provision has been made to limit the heat loss through the fabric of the building:
- Elemental method;
- Target U-value method; and
- Carbon Index method.

Elemental method (dwellings)
Whereas the Target U-value method and the Carbon Index method can be used with any heating system, the Elemental method can only be used when the heating system is based on an efficient gas or oil boiler, on a heat pump, on community heating with CHP or on biogas or biomass fuel, but not for direct electric heating or other systems. Reasonable provision for boiler efficiency can be demonstrated by using a boiler with a SEDBUK rating (Seasonal Efficiency of a Domestic Boiler in the UK) of no less than the values set out in ADL1 Table 2, i.e. 78 per cent for mains natural gas, 80 per cent for LPG and 85 per cent for oil fuelled boilers. Details of boiler efficiency ratings can be found at www.sedbuk.com.

The Elemental method is suitable for alterations and extension work, and for new-build work. When using the Elemental method, the requirement will be met for new dwellings by selecting construction elements that provide the U-value thermal performances given in ADL1 Table 1, reproduced below as Table 6, and the area of the windows, doors and roof lights together does not exceed 25 per cent of the total floor area.

❗ **If an area greater than 25 per cent of the floor area is required for window, doors, etc. then the Target U-value method should be used.**

Higher U-values than those shown in Table 6 may be allowed, but this will require further reduction in the area of glazing, which may result in unacceptably low levels of day lighting.

The use of the Elemental method minimises calculations, reduces the need for specialist input, such as from building services engineers, but also reduces the possibilities of trade-off between elements and reduces flexibility in design.

Work Stages: C, D and E

Table 6 Elemental method: U-values (W/m²K) for elements of construction
(taken from ADL1: Table 1 and ADL2: Table 1)

Building element		U-values L1	(W/m²K) L2
Floors:	ground and basement and floors over external spaces	0.25	0.25
Floors:	floors between heated and unheated internal space*	0.25	0.25
Walls:	including basement walls	0.35	0.35
Walls:	walls between heated and unheated internal space*	0.35	0.35
Roofs:	flat	0.25	0.25
	pitched: with insulation between rafters	0.20	0.20
	pitched: with integral insulation	0.25	0.25
	pitched: with insulation between joists	0.16	0.16
	pitched: with a pitch of 70° or more	0.35	0.35
Windows, doors and roof lights: glazing in metal frames		2.2	2.2
Windows, doors and roof lights: glazing in timber or PVC frames		2.0	2.0
Roof lights			2.2
Vehicle access and similar large doors			0.7

*For dwellings, elements exposed to the outside via an unheated space, the U-value should be determined using the method given in SAP 2001 For buildings other than dwellings, the unheated space may be disregarded so that the element is considered as directly exposed to the outside, or the U-value of the element may be calculated as the transmission heat loss coefficient through the unheated space divided by the area of the element. The transmission heat loss coefficient should be calculated as given in BS EN ISO 13789.

ADL1 sets out the following methods of achieving the U-values specified for elements of construction:

- For all elements, one method is by providing the thickness of insulation taken from the tables in Appendix A of the ADL1. The limitation in this case is that only certain constructional details are prescribed. For example, in the case of windows these tables could be used only where the windows are fitted within a frame.
- For walls and roofs, an alternative method is by calculating the U-value using the combined method of calculation outlined in Appendix B of the ADL1. This method is set out in greater detail in the CIBSE Guide Section A3 1999 edition.
- For floors, an alternative method is using the data given in the tables in Appendix C of the Approved Document.
- For basements, an alternative method is to follow the guidance which is given in the BCA/NHBC Approved Document *Basements for dwellings*.
- For doors, windows and roof lights, an average U-value which equals the U-value in Table B3.cde1 could be used if the combined area of those elements is no greater than 25 per cent of the total floor area of the dwelling. This would permit individual doors, windows or roof lights to have U-values that exceed the U-value standards of Table B3.cde1. Appendix D of the ADL1 gives examples of how average U-values are calculated.

Sections 0.11 to 0.13 of ADL1 give guidance as to official publications that can be used when calculating U-values. The BRE (2002) *Conventions for U-value Calculations* gives guidance on the relevant calculation procedures set out in the new standards and other documents.

Elemental method (extensions to dwellings)

The Regulations apply also to extensions to dwellings, and the Elemental method can be used to demonstrate reasonable provision for limiting heat loss in extensions, by applying the U-values in Table 6. Unlike the position with whole dwellings, some trade-off is possible between U-values for the different elements in extensions.

For small extensions, i.e. not more than 6 m² of heated areas, then reasonable provision would be for the energy performance of the elements of the extension to be no worse than those of the main house.

For doors, windows and roof lights within the extension, an average U-value which equals the U-value in Table 6 could be used if:
- the combined area of those elements is no greater than 25 per cent of the total floor area of the extension plus the area of any doors or windows which as a result of the extension are not exposed;
or
- the area of the doors, windows and roof lights of the enlarged dwelling is no greater than that of the doors, windows and roof lights of the dwelling without the extension; or
- the area of the doors, windows and roof lights of the enlarged dwelling is no greater than 25 per cent of the total floor area of the enlarged dwelling.

Whilst the Target U-value and Carbon Index methods may be used for extensions to dwellings, the extension and the rest of the house must be handled as one entity and the method applied to the whole enlarged dwelling.

Target U-value method (dwellings)

The Target U-value method can be used for complete dwellings and permits some flexibility in the choice of:
- total areas of doors, windows and roof lights;
- U-values of individual elements of construction; and
- efficiency of the heating system and type of fuel.

Compliance is deemed to have been achieved if the Target U-value is not less than the area-weighted average U-value of all the exposed elements of the dwelling. The Target U-value is calculated using a series of equations under Sections 1.18 through to 1.25 of the Approved Document L1. Appendix E of the Approved Document L1 gives worked examples in using the Target U-value method.

The method of calculation of the Target U-value allows for adjustments and it is these adjustments that bring flexibility to this method. The Target U-value needs to be adjusted to account for:
- heating system performance;
- window frame type; and
- solar gains achieved due to the building orientation (i.e. if the area of glazing on the south elevation exceeds that on the north, the Target U-values can be increased using an equation set out in the ADL1.

If more than one type of adjustment is applied, then that for solar glazing should be applied last.

Whilst the Target U-value method could result in some parts of construction elements having U-values which are worse than those in Table 6 (for example, one of the walls or a fireplace recess), ADL1 stipulates that the poorest acceptable U-value is 0.35 W/m²K for parts of roofs and 0.7 W/m²K for parts of exposed walls or floors.

Carbon Index method (dwellings)

This method can be used for complete dwellings and affords greater design flexibility than the other two methods by permitting trade-offs between areas of openings, heating systems, orientation, types of window frames, and U-values of construction elements.

Whilst the Carbon Index method could result in some parts of construction elements having U-values which are worse than those in Table B3.cde1 the poorest acceptable U-value for parts of walls is 0.35 W/m²K and 0.7 W/m²K for parts of exposed walls or floors.

Compliance is deemed to have been achieved if the Carbon Index for the dwelling is no less than 8.0. This is based on a scale between a Carbon Index of 0.0 and a Carbon Index of 10.0 where the higher the number the better the standard. The method that should be used to calculate the Carbon Index is detailed in the Government's Standard Assessment Procedure (SAP) for energy rating of dwellings. More information on SAP 2001 is given in the Chapter 7.

Limiting thermal bridging and air leakage (dwellings)

In order to meet the requirements of Part L, there should be no significant thermal bridges in the building fabric, and the building should be reasonably airtight, meaning that there should be a

Work Stages: C, D and E

continuous air barrier in contact with the insulation over the whole thermal envelope. The Approved Document L1 suggests that this can done by:
- adopting recommendations in the supporting publication, *Limiting thermal bridging and air leakage: Robust construction details for dwellings and similar buildings;* or
- demonstrating by calculation or by testing that the building's performance is as good as the 'Robust construction details'. In the case of thermal bridges, BRE Information Paper IP 17/01 may be used for this purpose. For air leakage, the building would need to be pressure tested following the method given in CIBSE TM 23 and the air permeability of the building should not exceed the level indicated in Section 1.35 of ADL1.

❗ **In dealing with the requirements of Part L1 for airtightness, regard must be given to the requirements of Part F, in relation to the need to provide adequate ventilation for health, and to Part J, in relation to the need to provide adequate air for combustion appliances.**

Limiting heat losses: Insulation of pipes and ducts (dwellings)

The requirement for limiting heat loss from hot water pipes and hot air ducts used for space heating can be met by providing adequate insulation. The ADL1 gives guidance to some ways of meeting the requirement for insulating pipes and ducts:
- space heating pipe work located outside the building fabric insulation layers should be insulated with material having a thermal conductivity at 40°C not exceeding 0.035 W/mK and a thickness equal to the outside diameter of the pipe up to a maximum of 40 mm; or
- for pipes and in the case of warm air ducts providing insulation in accordance with the recommendations of BS 5422:2001, *Methods for specifying thermal insulation materials on pipes, ductwork and equipment in the temperature range –40°C to +700°C;*
- insulating the hot pipes connected to hot water storage vessels, including the vent pipe, and the primary flow and return to the heat exchanger, where fitted, to the standard in (b) above for at least 1 metre from their points of connection (or they should be insulated up to the point where they become concealed); and
- in unheated areas central heating and hot water pipe work may need increased insulation thicknesses for protection against freezing. Guidance on this is given in BRE Report No 262 *Thermal insulation: avoiding risks.*

Heating and lighting systems (dwellings)

In addition to making reasonable provision for limiting the heat loss through the fabric of the building and from hot water systems, Part L1 of the Regulations also requires that provision shall be made for the conservation of fuel and power in dwellings by:
- providing space heating and hot water systems which are energy efficient;
- providing lighting systems with appropriate lamps and sufficient controls so that energy can be used efficiently.

Hot water systems (dwellings)

The ADL1 notes that there are several acceptable ways for limiting heat loss from hot water systems and for such systems to be energy efficient:
- for systems incorporating integral or separate hot water storage vessels, the possible ways include:
    (i) the hot water storage systems to meet the insulation requirements of BS 1566, BS 699, BS 3198 or BS 7206;
    (ii) the hot water vessel to have a 35 mm thick, factory applied coating of PU-foam having a minimum density of 30 kg/m^3;
- for indirectly heated hot water storage systems, the heat exchanger to be at least the same size as that recommended in BS 1566, BS 3198 or BS 7206 and be served by a pumped primary system; and
- for primary storage systems, the system to meet the requirements of the Waterheater Manufacturers Association's performance specification for thermal stores.

Mechanical systems (dwellings)

Demonstrating that the space and water heating systems are reasonably energy efficient can be done by including temperature zone controls, timing controls and boiler control interlocks. An acceptable system configuration would be one that can:

- zone areas according to their heating needs, such as living and sleeping, and use temperature sensing devices such as room thermostats or thermostatic radiator valves to control the room temperature;
- in the case of most dwellings, has one timing zone which can be divided into two temperature sub-zones. No zone should have an area greater than 150 m²;
- control the time period when the heating systems operate;
- provide separate time controls for the space heating and water heating (exceptions include combination boilers and solid fuel appliances);
- switch gas and oil fired boiler off when heat is not required irrespective of other temperature controls within the system.

An alternative method to show compliance would be to adopt the recommendations of BS 5864 or of the Good Practice Guide 302 and include zoning, timing and interlock features similar to the above.

Artificial lighting (dwellings)

The requirement for providing efficient internal lighting with appropriate lamps could be met by having fixed lighting in a number of suitable locations, that only takes energy efficient lamps. Lamp details and guidance on locations are given in Sections 1.54 to 1.56 of the Approved Document L1. Table 4 of the Approved Document gives the minimum number of locations (a minimum of one location per three rooms), or alternatively, guidance is given in the General Information Leaflet 20: *Low energy domestic lighting.*

Where external lights are used these should automatically switch off when there is enough daylight and when not required, or have fixed lighting that only take energy efficient lamps. Lamp details are given in Section 1.57 of the ADL1.

Part L2 (buildings other than dwellings)

The ADL2 gives three methods which could be used to demonstrate that reasonable provision has been made for the conservation of fuel and power.

(a) Elemental method;
(b) Whole-building method; and
(c) Carbon emissions calculation method.

These different methods offer increasing design flexibility in return for greater demands in terms of the extent of calculation required. However the overall aim is to achieve the same standard in terms of carbon emissions.

Elemental method (buildings other than dwellings)

The Elemental method for buildings other than dwellings offers some design flexibility by permitting limited trade-off between elements of construction, insulation levels and heating system performance.

To show compliance using the Elemental method for buildings other than dwellings, the building envelope must meet minimum U-values, and the building services systems must meet minimum standards of energy efficiency.

U-values for construction elements

ADL2 sets out the following methods of showing that the envelope meets the minimum U-values shown in Table 6:
- for all elements, one method is by providing the thickness of insulation taken from the tables in the ADL2 Appendix A. The limitation in this case is that only certain constructional details are prescribed. For example, in the case of windows, these tables could be used only where the windows are fitted within a frame.
- for floors, an alternative method is to use data given in ADL2 Appendix C.

The method provides some trade-offs between elements of construction, insulation levels and heating system performance, as set out in ADL2 paragraphs 1.14 and 1.32. However paragraph 1.16 imposes limits as to what is considered acceptable in the scope and scale of such trade-offs (see Table 7). Other design constraints, such as the need to provide adequate daylight, will also limit the extent to which the trade-off can be used.

The methods to be used in calculating U-values are set out in Appendix B to ADL2. The BRE (2002) *Conventions for U-value Calculations* gives guidance on the relevant calculation procedures set out in the new standards and other documents.

Work Stages: C, D and E

Table 7 Limitations on Elemental method trade-offs (buildings other than dwellings)

Element	Limitations	Guidance
Openings: windows, doors and roof lights (Building type dependant)	Maximum acceptable areas as percentage of walls and of roofs (unless compensating measures are taken)	ADL2 paras. 1.12 to 1.14 and Table 2
Openings: glazing (Orientation dependant)	Maximum acceptable area of opening as a percentage of the internal area	ADL2 paras. 1.20 to 1.23 and Table 4
Roofs, walls and floors	Poorest acceptable U-value	ADL2 paras. 1.14, 1.15 and Table 3
Heating system (Fuel dependant)	Maximum allowable carbon intensities as a percentage of the maximum heat output of the heating system	ADL2 paras. 1.25 to 1.26, 1.32 and Table 5

Limiting thermal bridging and air leakage

The requirements that there should be no significant thermal bridges in the building fabric, and the building should be reasonably airtight, can be met by having a continuous air barrier in contact with the insulation over the whole thermal envelope. The Approved Document L2 suggests that for this can done by:
- adopting, for 'domestic type' construction only, recommendations in the governmental report, *Limiting thermal bridging and air leakage: Robust construction details for dwellings and similar buildings;* or
- demonstrating by calculation or by adopting robust design practices that the building's performance is as good as the 'Robust construction details'. In the case of thermal bridges, BRE Information Paper IP 17/01 and MRCMA Technical Report N014 may be used for this purpose, with the latter also giving guidance for airtightness.

In dealing with the requirements of Part L2 for air tightness, regard must be given to the requirements of Part F, in relation to the need to provide adequate ventilation for health, and to Part J, in relation to the need to provide adequate air for combustion appliances.

Limiting exposure to solar overheating

The requirement to limit exposure to solar overheating in the building may be met through:
- the use of appropriate type glazing;
- the use of passive measures such as shading;
- the use of exposed thermal capacity combined with night ventilation (detailed guidance being given in GIR 31).

A way of achieving compliance for spaces that have single orientation glazing is to follow the limits on the allowable area of such glazing set out in ADL2 Table 4. The area of glazed opening is expressed as a percentage of the internal area of that element, and varies from 12 per cent for horizontal roof lights to 50 per cent for north facing walls.

ADL2 paragraph 1.23 refers to two alternative procedures that can be used to demonstrate compliance:
- using a procedure described in ADL2 Appendix H, compliance would be deemed if the solar heat load per unit floor area averaged between the hours of 07:30 and 17:30 is no greater than 25 W/m^2;
- using detailed calculation procedures such as those described in Chapter 5 of CIBSE Guide A, compliance would be deemed if, without mechanical cooling or mechanical ventilation, the space does not overheat when subjected to an internal gain of 10 W/m^2.

Heating systems

Regulation L2(c) requires that space heating and hot water systems are energy efficient. Methods of demonstrating compliance with this requirement are set out in Table 8.

Table 8 Acceptable standards for heating and hot water system (buildings other than dwellings)

Element	Guidance
Heating The requirements can be met by showing that the carbon intensity of the heat generating equipment at maximum heat output of the system and at 30 per cent of heat output of the system are not greater than the values shown in ADL2 Table 5. The carbon intensity is based on the carbon emitted per useful kWh of heat output. ADL2 paragraphs 1.27–1.30 set out methods for calculating the carbon intensity of individual and multiple boilers, heat pumps, electrical heating, combined heat and power systems and community heating. Trade-off between the carbon intensity of the heating system and the average U-value of the envelope is permissible provided that the rate of carbon emissions remains unchanged. ADL2 paragraph 1.32 describes the method to be used for adjusting the average U-value of the envelope to facilitate such trade-off.	ADL2 paras. 1.24 to 1.32, Tables 5 and 6
Hot water The requirements can be met by: ● avoiding over-sized hot water storage systems ● avoiding low-load operation of heat raising plant ● avoiding the use of grid supplied electric water heating except where hot water demand is low ● providing solar water heating ● minimising the length of circulation loops ● minimising the length and diameter of dead legs within the system	ADL2 para. 1.35
Controls In the case of space heating, the requirements can be met by providing zone, timing and temperature controls so that each functional area can be maintained at the required temperature. The controls should be able to have the heating systems come on only during the occupation of the building. For extended hours of occupation and for provision of sufficient heating to prevent condensation or frost damage when the heating system would otherwise be switched off, additional controls would be needed. For hot water storage systems, the controls should be able to shut off the heating when the required water temperature is achieved and during periods when hot water is not required. For small buildings with a heating system maximum output not exceeding 100 kW, guidance given in GPG 132 should be followed, whilst for larger or more complex buildings, guidance given in CIBSE Guide H should be followed.	ADL2 paras. 1.36 and 1.37
Insulation to pipework, ductwork and storage vessels The requirements can be met by insulating pipework, ductwork and storage vessels to BS 5422. In cases where the heat flow through the walls of the pipe, duct or vessel is always useful in conditioning the surrounding space when fluid is flowing through the pipe or duct or is being stored, then insulation would not be required under the regulations.	ADL2 paras. 1.38 to 1.40

Table 9 Acceptable standards for lighting systems

Lighting use	Acceptable standard	Guidance
General lighting in office, industrial and storage building types	Provide lighting with an initial efficacy averaged over the whole building of not less than 40 luminaire-lumens/circuit-watt.	ADL2 paras. 1.43 to 1.47 and Table 7
General lighting in other building types (not dwellings)	Installed lighting capacity which has an initial (100 hour) lamp plus ballast efficacy of not less than 50 lamp-lumens/circuit-watt. A way of achieving this would be to provide at least 95 per cent of the installed lighting capacity using lamps with circuit efficacies no worse than those in Table 8 of ADL2	ADL2 paras. 1.48 to 1.49, Tables 8 and 9
Display lighting in all buildings (not dwellings)	Installed lighting capacity which has an initial (100 hour) lamp plus ballast efficacy of not less than 50 lamp-lumens/circuit-watt. A way of achieving this installed capacity of display lighting averaged over the building has an initial (100 hour) efficacy of not less than 15 lamp-lumens/circuit-watt. In calculating this efficacy, the power consumed by any transformers or ballasts should be taken into account.	ADL2 paras. 1.50 to 1.52 and Table 10

Table 10 Acceptable standards for lighting controls

Lighting controls	Acceptable standard	Guidance
Controls in office and storage building types	Provision of local switches in easily accessible positions within each working area or at boundaries between working areas and general circulation routes.	ADL2 paras. 1.56 and 1.57
Controls in other building types (not dwellings)	Provide one or more of the following types of control system arranged to maximise the beneficial use of daylight: (a) local switching as described in ADL2 para. 1.57; (b) time switching; (c) photo-electric switching.	ADL2 para. 1.58
Controls for display lighting in all buildings (not dwellings)	Connected in dedicated circuits that can be switched off at times when people will not be inspecting exhibits or merchandise or being entertained.	ADL2 para. 1.59

Lighting
The requirements of the regulations would be met if the lighting systems are reasonably efficient and make effective use of daylight where appropriate. Methods of demonstrating compliance with this requirement are set out in Table 9.

❗ **Emergency escape lighting and special process lighting are not subject to the requirements of Part L. (Special process lighting is defined in ADL 1.53 (b) as lighting intended to illuminate specialist tasks within a space, rather than the space itself, e.g., theatre spotlights or medical lighting in operating theatres.)**

Lighting controls
The requirements of the regulations would be met if the lighting controls encourage the maximum use of daylight and avoid unnecessary lighting during unoccupied times without endangering the safe passage of the people. Methods of demonstrating compliance with this requirement are set out in Table 10.

Air conditioning and mechanical ventilation (ACMV)
The regulations require that for buildings other than dwellings, reasonable provision for the conservation of fuel and power shall be made by:

> ...making provision where air conditioning and mechanical ventilation systems are installed, so that no more energy needs to be used than is reasonable in the circumstances.

ADL2 states that buildings with ACMV would comply with the regulations if designed and constructed so that:
- the form and fabric of the building do not result in a need for excessive installed capacity of ACMV equipment. Particularly, the use of appropriate glazing ratios and solar shading methods are important ways to limit cooling needs.
- fans, pumps and refrigeration equipment are reasonably efficient and appropriately sized to have no more capacity for demand and stand by than is necessary for the task.
- suitable facilities are provided to manage, control and monitor the operation of the equipment and the systems.

For office buildings, a means of showing compliance is to demonstrate that the Carbon Performance Rating is satisfactory (the method of calculation is set out in Appendix G to ADL2). This does not apply where there are innovative features in the design, where the carbon emissions calculations method should be used. Lesser standards are required when extending or replacing existing ACMV systems.

For buildings other than offices, ADL2 states 'it is only possible at present to define an overall performance requirement' which it sets out in the form of specific fan power values, relating the capacity of the installed fans to the volume of air supplied and extracted.

Methods of demonstrating compliance with this requirement for reasonably efficient ACMV systems are set out in Table 11.

Whole-building method (buildings other than dwellings)
The Whole-building method allows for more design flexibility than the Elemental method by considering energy performance of the building as a whole. The aim is to show that the level of carbon emissions or primary energy consumption at the whole building level is within acceptable levels. The ADL2 offers guidance for three building types: offices, schools and hospitals (see Table 12).

Carbon emissions calculation method (buildings other than dwellings)
This method considers the performance of the whole building, but unlike the Whole-building method which has limited building type applicability, this method can be applied to any building type. The method also allows more design flexibility by taking into account a number of energy conservation measures and the effects of useful solar gains and occupancy heat gains.

To demonstrate compliance, the building's annual carbon emissions should be no greater than that from a notional building, of the same size and shape, that meets the compliance criteria of the Elemental method. The carbon emissions from the proposed building and the notional building need to be calculated using an approved thermal model. ADL2 paragraph 1.76 gives details as to how a thermal model may be given approval and gives guidance on the constraints that need to be taken into account when using this method. CIBSE AM11 *Building Energy and Environmental Modelling* gives guidance on the selection of appropriate software for use with this method.

Through the legislation maze: energy conservation

Table 11 Acceptable standards for ACMV

Building type	Acceptable standard	Guidance
Office	Carbon Performance Rating (CPR) should be no greater than values given in ADL2 Table 11	ADL2 paras. 1.62 to 1.66. Table 11 and Appendix G
Other building types (not dwellings)	The specific fan power (SFP) is less than the values given in the ADL2 para. 1.67(a) and (b) and provision of efficient variable flow control systems	ADL2 paras. 1.67 to 1.68

Definitions of terms related to ACMV are given in ADL2 paragraphs 1.60 and 1.61.

Table 12 Guidance for offices, schools and hospitals

Building type	Acceptable standard	Guidance
Offices	The whole-office CPR is no greater than the values shown in ADL2 Table 12; and the envelope is reasonably airtight, demonstrated by meeting the requirements of ADL2 paras. 1.9 to 1.11, 1.17 to 1.19 and Table 3.	ADL2 paras. 1.9 to 1.11, 1.17 to 1.19, 1.62 to 1.66, Tables 11 and 12, Appendix G. BRE Digest No 457.
Schools	To conform with the DfEE *Guidelines for environmental design in schools,* Building Bulletin 87, TSO	ADL2 para. 1.72, DfEE 1997: *Guidelines for environmental design in schools,* Building Bulletin 87, TSO
Hospitals	To conform with NHS Estates' guide, *Achieving energy efficiency in new hospitals*	ADL2 para. 1.73, NHS Estates, 1994: *Achieving energy efficiency in new hospitals,* TSO

Conservatories, atria and similar sun-spaces

The Approved Documents L1 and L2 define a conservatory (or a sun-space in ADL2) as being a building or part of a building that:

> ... has not less than three-quarters of the area of its roof and not less than one half of the area of its external walls made of translucent material.

Where there is no separation between the conservatory and the building (or dwelling in ADL1), the conservatory should be treated as an integral part of the building.

Where there is separation between the conservatory and the building, the conservatory may be left unheated, or if fixed heating installations are to be included then they should have their own separate temperature and on/off controls. The element of the structure separating the conservatory from the building, be it a floor, wall, window or door, should have the same U-value and energy performance as the equivalent element in the rest of the building.

In cases where an opening is formed or enlarged between a conservatory and an existing building, the existing separation where the opening is not to be enlarged should be retained, or separation should be provided which has a U-value equivalent to the U-value standard of windows and doors in Table 1 of the Approved Documents L1 and L2.

References and further reading

BRE, 2002: Report No 262, *Thermal insulation: avoiding risks.*

BRE 2002: *Conventions for U-value Calculations.*

BRE Digest 457: *The Carbon Performance Rating for Offices.*

BRE IP 17/01: *Assessing the effects of thermal bridging at junctions and around openings in the external elements of buildings.*

BRESCU, 2001: Good Practice Guide 302, *Controls for domestic central heating and hot water*, Garston, Watford.

BRESCU/DEFRA/DTLR, 2002: SAP 2001, *The Government's Standard Assessment Procedure for Energy Rating of Dwellings,* Garston, Watford.

BS 5422: 2001: *Methods for specifying thermal insulation materials on pipes, ductwork and equipment in the temperature range -40°C to +700°C.*

BS 5864: 1989: *Specification for installation in domestic premises of gas-fired ducted air heaters of rated output not exceeding 60 kW.*

CIBSE, 1998, AM11: *Building Energy and Environmental Modelling.*

CIBSE, 1999: *Guide A, Environmental design.*

CIBSE, 2000: Guide H, *Building Control Systems.*

CIBSE, 2000: TM 23, *Testing buildings for air leakage,* Chartered Institute of Building Services Engineers, London.

DEFRA/DTLR 2001: *Limiting thermal bridging and air leakage: Robust construction details for dwellings and similar buildings.*

DfEE, 1997: *Guidelines for environmental design in schools,* Building Bulletin 87, TSO.

Energy Efficiency Best Practice programme, 1995: GIR 31, *Avoiding or minimising the use of air-conditioning,* TSO.

GIL 20, 1995: *Low energy domestic lighting,* BRESCU.

GPG 132, 2001: *Energy Efficiency Best Practice Programme, Heating controls in small commercial and multi-residential buildings*, BRESCU.

GPG 303, 2000: *The designer's guide to energy efficient buildings for industry, Energy Efficiency Best practice programme*, BRESCU.

MCRMA, 2002: *Technical Note 14, Guidance for the design of metal cladding and roofing to comply with the Approved Document L.*

NHS Estates, 1994: *Achieving energy efficiency in new hospitals,* TSO.

Waterheater Manufacturers Association, 1999: *Performance specification for thermal stores.*

6. Work Stages: F, G and H

Production Information
Tender Documents
Tender Action

During the working drawings stage, care will need to be taken that all decisions made regarding the design are carried through into the production information.

For satisfactory design details, the Approved Documents L1 and L2 refer to a DEFRA/DTLR publication *Limiting thermal bridging and air leakage: Robust construction details for dwellings and similar buildings.* If these are to be used as a method of meeting the requirements, they will need to be incorporated into the production information package and integrated with the rest of the design.

Although the 'Robust Construction Details' may satisfy Parts L1 and L2 requirements for limiting thermal bridging and air leakage, they may not necessarily satisfy other aspects of the building regulations (e.g. water ingress) or the requirements of the particular project, so their incorporation should be treated with care.

During the preparation of the production information and tender documents, careful coordination will be required to ensure that the regulations are met. As pointed out under 'to whom do the regulations apply', it is in the client's interests to ensure that the specific duties are clearly allocated amongst those who are engaged to carry out the building project.

For example, where a contractor or sub-contractor is designing a part of a building under a design portion supplement (or a specialist M&E sub-contractor is designing a heating system) it will be important to ensure that they design according to the provisions of Part L, and provide their detailed design information in sufficient time for the person who is coordinating the design to ensure overall compliance.

Most standard forms of contract place a general duty on the contractor to comply with relevant legislation. Nevertheless, if it is the intention that the contractor or a sub-contractor takes on specific responsibilities relating to Part L, H or J (for example, any of the tasks listed under 'additional checks by builders' in the Approved Documents), then these should be included as a contractor obligation within the tender documents.

Of particular relevance are the new requirements for testing, commissioning and certification (see Table 13). Depending on the building type and the methods selected to demonstrate compliance, extensive testing could be required during the period leading up to Practical Completion. Provision should be made in the production information and contract documents, and adequate resources allowed. Some of these requirements for testing are discussed below, and further guidance can be found in the useful publication BRESCU General Information Report 64: *Post-construction testing – a professional's guide to testing housing for energy efficiency.*

Continuity of insulation

The regulations require, for all building types, that measures are taken to avoid thermal bridging or gaps in the insulation. Under ADL1 Compliance with this requirement must be shown through the use of 'robust details' or by calculation. No certificates or declarations are required with respect to thermal bridging in dwellings. Under ADL2 only, one method of demonstrating that thermal bridging has been avoided is through infra-red thermography inspection. If this is to be used it should be carried out according to the Guidance in BRE Report 176: *A practical guide for infra-red thermography for building surveys.* The alternative method is through the use of appropriate design details and building techniques. Whichever method is used, a certificate or declaration of compliance must be obtained from a suitably qualified person (see Table 13).

Note that the use of thermography inspection is not cited in ADL1 as a method of demonstrating compliance for dwellings, which must be shown through the use of 'robust details' or by calculation (see Table 13). A certificate or declaration is not required.

Work Stages: F, G and H

Air leakage tests

The Approved Documents state that to satisfy the requirements of the regulations, air leakage through the building fabric should be reduced (in the case of dwellings) and minimised (in the case of buildings other than dwellings).

ADL2 requires that air leakage tests are carried out on all buildings of more than 1000 m^2 gross floor area. The pressure tests should be carried out in accordance with CIBSE TM 23: *Testing buildings for air leakage*. This method can also be used as an alternative to using 'robust details' to demonstrate compliance for dwellings, and other buildings of less than 1000 m^2. For buildings other than dwellings, a certificate or declaration is required in relation to the minimising of air infiltration (see Table 13). A certificate or declaration is not required for dwellings, although it might be sensible to obtain one where air leakage tests are conducted.

Commissioning of systems

Both Approved Documents L1 and L2 require that commissioning of mechanical systems should be carried out. Under ADL1 it states that heating and hot water systems 'should be commissioned to make reasonably certain that they can operate efficiently for the purposes of the conservation of fuel and power'. ADL2 simply states that 'in the context of building services systems, "providing", or "making provision" should be taken as including, where relevant, inspection and commissioning'.

The term 'commissioning' is defined in both parts as:

> The advancement of these systems from the state of static completion to working order to the specifications relevant to achieving compliance with Part L, without prejudice to the need to comply with health and safety requirements.

And for each system the following should be included:
- setting-to-work;
- regulation (testing and adjusting repetitively) to achieve the specified performance;
- calibration, setting up and testing of the associated automatic control system;
- recording of the system settings and the performance test results that have been accepted as satisfactory.

Both Approved Documents state that responsibility for achieving compliance rests with the 'person carrying out the work', who may be a developer or main contractor or a sub-contractor or a specialist firm directly appointed by the client.

Under ADL1, this person should either themselves provide a certificate, or obtain a certificate from the sub-contractor, that commissioning has been successfully carried out. The certificate should be made available to the client and the building control body. Where the person giving the certificate has a recognised qualification, the certificate may be accepted by the building control body as evidence that the relevant requirements in Part L1 (b) and (d) have been complied with. If there is no relevant qualification, or if a suitably qualified certifier is not available, the person responsible for carrying out the work should nevertheless provide or obtain a written declaration of successful commissioning and make it available to the client and the building control body (see Table 13).

Under ADL2 the person responsible for achieving compliance should provide a report, or obtain one from a suitable qualified person, that indicates that the inspection and commissioning activities necessary to demonstrate that the work complies with Part L have been completed to a reasonable standard (see Table 13).

❗ If relying on the use of registered or approved persons to achieve exemption from the requirement to give notice/deposit plans (under Regulation 12(5), or the use of certificated of FESNA registered persons as proof of compliance with Regulations 6 and 7 (under Regulation 16A), then the use of such persons must be made clear in the tender documents.

Local Authority tests

Note that under new Regulation 18 the Local Authority may make such tests of any building as may be necessary to establish whether it complies. It may be sensible to include some provision for attendance by the contractor should the Local Authority decide to conduct such tests.

Work Stages: F, G and H

Table 13 Declarations/certificates and reports

Element	Requirement	Statement and/or inclusions	Guidance
Continuity of insulation – buildings other than dwellings	Certificate or declaration by a suitably qualified person	To state: • that appropriate design details and building techniques have been used and that the work has been carried out in ways that can be expected to achieve reasonable conformity with the specifications that have been approved for the purposes of compliance with Part L2; **or** • that infra-red thermography inspections have shown that the insulation is reasonably continuous over the whole visible envelope	ADL2 para. 2.1 BRE Report 176
Airtightness – buildings other than dwellings	Certificate or declaration by a suitably qualified person	To state: • for buildings of any size, that the results of air leakage tests carried out in accordance with CIBSE TM 23 are satisfactory; **or** • for buildings of less than 1000 m^2 gross floor area, that appropriate design details and building techniques have been used, and that the work has been carried out in ways that can be expected to achieve reasonable conformity with the specifications that have been approved for the purposes of compliance with Part L2	ADL2 para.2.2 CIBSE TM 23
Commissioning of heating and hot water systems – dwellings	Certificate or declaration by a suitably qualified person, or a declaration by the person carrying out the work	To state: • that commissioning has been successfully carried out	ADL1 para. 1.49 Benchmark Code of Practice for the Installation, Commissioning and Servicing of Central Heating Systems.
Commissioning of building services systems – buildings other than dwellings	Report by a suitably qualified person	To include: • a commissioning plan that shows that every system has been inspected and commissioned in an appropriate sequence. (A way of demonstrating compliance would be to follow the guidance in the CIBSE Commissioning Codes and BSRIA Commissioning Guides), and: • the results of the tests confirming that the performance is reasonably in accordance with the approved designs including written commentaries where exclusions are proposed to be accepted	ADL2 paras. 2.5 to 2.7 CIBSE Commissioning Codes and BSRIA Commissioning Guides

Work Stages: F, G and H

Notices

Approved Documents J, H and L require Notices to be fixed within the building. The details of such Notices are given in the next chapter (Work Stage J, K, and L). If it is the intention that the contractor should be responsible for producing and affixing such Notices then these requirements should be made explicit at Tender Stage.

References and further reading

BRE, 1991: BRE report 176, *A practical guide to infra-red thermography for building surveys.*

BRESCU General Information Report 64: *Post-construction testing – a professional's guide to testing housing for energy efficiency.*

CIBSE, 2000: TM 23, *Testing buildings for air leakage. Chartered Institute of Building Services Engineers, London.*

DEFRA/DTLR, 2001: *Limiting thermal bridging and air leakage: Robust construction details for dwellings and similar buildings.*

7. Work Stages: J, K and L

Mobilisation
Practical Completion and After

During these stages it is important to ensure that the Part L requirements for commissioning, testing and certification are met. These were dealt with in the previous chapter due to the need to make provision for them in the production information. Equally important at this stage are the Part L requirements for provision of instructions, information and the posting of Notices, which are dealt with below.

Operating and Maintenance instructions for building services

Regulations L1(d) and L2(h) require that sufficient information should be provided with the heating and hot water systems (or relevant services in L2) so that building occupiers can operate and maintain the services (in the case of L2 '…the building can be operated and maintained…') in such a manner as to use no more energy than is reasonable in the circumstances.

ADL1 offers very little guidance in relation to this, simply noting that:
- such information should be given to the building owner;
- the operating and maintenance instructions should be in an accessible format;
- such instructions should be provided for each new dwelling and for whenever the systems are altered;
- the instructions should be specific to the installed system;
- the instructions should explain how the system can be operated so that it can perform efficiently; and
- routine maintenance requirements specific for the conservation of fuel and power should be provided.

ADL2 describes in some detail the type of information that should be provided. Such information should be provided through the use of a building log-book and through the installation of energy supply meters.

Building log-book

The information provided in the building log-book should be provided in summary form and could refer to other project documentation, such as the Operation and Maintenance manual and the Health and Safety file. ADL2 paragraph 3.2 lists the information that the building log-book could provide:
- description of the building, its use, design philosophy and its services systems;
- schedule of the floor areas of each of the building zones categorised by environmental servicing type (e.g. airconditioned, naturally ventilated);
- location of the relevant plant and equipment, including simplified schematic diagrams;
- installed capacities (input power and output rating) of the services plant;
- simple descriptions of the operational and control strategies of the energy consuming services in the building;
- copy of declarations covering air tightness and commissioning of systems (see Chapter 6);
- operating and maintenance instructions that include provisions enabling the specified performance to be sustained during occupation;
- schedule of the building's energy supply meters, giving information on the type of fuel that each meters, their location, identification and description, and instructions on their use;
- for offices of 200 m^2 and over, a design assessment of the building services systems' carbon emissions and the comparable performance benchmark (guidance is given in ADL2 Appendix G).

Energy supply meters

Energy supply meters should be provided together with instructions giving a metering strategy (for guidance see BRESCU: GIL 65), explaining how to attribute energy consumptions to end uses and how to compare operating performances with published benchmarks. This will often involve directly or indirectly metering boiler, chiller and fan installations together with distribution boards. ADL2 paragraphs 3.3 to 3.6 give guidance on the type of metering provisions that would satisfy the requirements.

Work Stages: J, K and L

Notices

Energy rating of dwellings

Under Regulation 16 of the Building Regulations 2000 (see Figure 2), in the case of a new dwelling the energy rating of that dwelling must be calculated using a procedure which is approved by the Secretary of State, the local authority must be given notice of that rating, and a notice stating the energy rating of the dwelling must be displayed in a conspicuous place in the dwelling.

❗ Where a person creates a new dwelling (by work or material change of use), but intends to occupy the dwelling as a residence, then the person is not required to affix a notice but must still calculate the SAP rating and notify this to the local authority.

SAP 2001

Currently the only approved procedure is the Government's Standard Assessment Procedure 2001, known as SAP 2001, version 9.70 (the current version published in early 2002, includes corrections to the earlier 2001 edition). The main changes in SAP 2001 are the following:

- the Carbon Index (CI) is now included. This is expressed on a scale of 0.0 to 10.0, the higher the number the better the performance;
- the upper limit of the SAP rating has been raised from 100 to 120. The range is now 1 to 120;
- both the SAP rating and the CI are adjusted for floor area in order to make them less dependant on the size of the dwelling;
- the U-values in the calculations are based on European Standards;
- a number of additional heating systems are included; and
- data tables have been updated.

SAP 2001 version 9.70 should be followed if the Carbon Index method is chosen as a way of demonstrating that reasonable provision has been made to limit the heat loss through the fabric of a dwelling. Details about the Carbon Index method are given in Chapter 5 (C, D and E) of this Guide.

Energy rating notices

Once the energy rating is calculated using SAP 2001, a notice of that rating must be given to the local authority. This can be done at any time during

Figure 2: Energy rating (Building Regulations 2000) Regulation 16

> (1) This regulation applies where a new dwelling is created by building work or by a material change of use in connection with which building work is carried out.
> (2) Where this regulation applies, the person carrying out the building work shall calculate the energy rating of the dwelling by means of a procedure approved by the Secretary of State and give notice of that rating to the local authority.
> (3) The notice referred to in paragraph (2) shall be given not later than the date on which the notice required by paragraph (4) of regulation 15 is given, and, where a new dwelling is created by the erection of a building, it shall be given at least five days before occupation of the dwelling.
> (4) Where this regulation applies, subject to paragraphs (6) and (7), the person carrying out the building work shall affix, as soon as practicable, in a conspicuous place in the dwelling, a notice stating the energy rating of the dwelling.
> (5) The notice referred to in paragraph (4) shall be affixed not later than the date on which the notice required by paragraph (4) of regulation 15 is given, and, where a new dwelling is created by the erection of a building, it shall be affixed not later than five days before occupation of the dwelling.
> (6) Subject to paragraph (7), if, on the date the dwelling is first occupied as a residence, no notice has been affixed in the dwelling in accordance with paragraph (4), the person carrying out the building work shall, not later than the date on which the notice required by paragraph (4) of regulation 15 is given, give to the occupier of the dwelling a notice stating the energy rating of the dwelling calculated in accordance with paragraph (2).
> (7) Paragraphs (4) and (6) shall not apply in a case where the person carrying out the work intends to occupy, or occupies, the dwelling as a residence.

the building process but no later than five days before completion of the works. A notice stating the energy rating of the dwelling has to be displayed in a conspicuous place in the dwelling no later than five days before completion of the works.

A suggested format for the notice is given in Circular 07/2000. This needs to be amended to account for the latest amendments to the building regulations and for SAP 2001. A suggestion for the amended format is shown in Figure 3.

If a notice has not been affixed as required by Regulation 16(4), the energy rating notice is to be given to the occupier rather than being posted in the dwelling. Circular 07/2000 suggests that this should contain the information shown in Figure 4.

Wastewater system notices

Part H requires that Notices should be fixed within the building describing the necessary maintenance of wastewater systems. Examples of the wording for such notices are shown in Figure 5.

References and further reading

Benchmark Code of Practice for the Installation, *Commissioning and Servicing of Central Heating Systems,* Central Heating Information Council.

BRE, 2001: *The Government's Standard Assessment Procedure for Energy Rating of Dwellings,* BRESCU, Garston, Watford.

BRE: *Air tightness in commercial and public buildings,* Building Research Establishment Report, BRE, Garston, Watford.

BRESCU General Information Report 64: *Post-construction testing - a professional's guide to testing housing for energy efficiency.*

BRESCU, 2001: GIL 65, *Sub metering new build non-domestic buildings.*

CIBSE, 2000: TM 23, *Testing buildings for air leakage.*

DEFRA/DTLR, 2001: *Limiting thermal bridging and air leakage: Robust construction details for dwellings and similar buildings.*

DETR Governmental Circular 07/2000.

Figure 3: Energy rating notice for posting in a dwelling (Regulation 16(4))

The energy rating of this dwelling is: **[figure on a scale of 1 to 120]**
[OR]
The energy rating of this dwelling is no worse than: **[figure on a scale of 1 to 120]**

This rating has been calculated in accordance with Building Regulations by **[or]** for **[name of company or person carrying out the building work]**, using the Government's Standard Assessment Procedure 2001 for Energy Rating of Dwellings ('SAP 2001').

A SAP energy rating gives a measure of the overall energy efficiency of a home. It is based on energy costs for space and water heating in the home. It is expressed on a scale of 1 to 120, the higher the number, the more energy efficient the dwelling.

For more information on SAP 2001 (and on energy efficiency more generally) contact your local Energy Efficiency Advice Centre on 0800 512012

Work Stages: J, K and L

Figure 4: Notification of energy rating to the occupier (Regulation 16(6))

> To the occupier **[or]** Name of occupier **[if known]**
> Property address
>
> Dear Sir or Madam **[or]** name of occupier,
>
> ENERGY RATING
>
> The energy rating of this dwelling is: **[figure on a scale of 1 to 120]**
> **[OR]**
> The energy rating of this dwelling is no worse than: **[figure on a scale of 1 to 120]**
>
> This rating has been calculated in accordance with Building Regulations by **[or]** for **[name of company or person carrying out the building work]**, using the Government's Standard Assessment Procedure 2001 for Energy Rating of Dwellings ('SAP 2001').
>
> A SAP energy rating gives a measure of the overall energy efficiency of a home. It is based on energy costs for space and water heating in the home. It is expressed on a scale of 1 to 120, the higher the number, the more energy efficient the dwelling.
>
> For more information on SAP 2001 (and on energy efficiency more generally) contact your local Energy Efficiency Advice Centre on 0800 512012.
>
> Yours faithfully **[or]** sincerely,
>
>
> **[person, or representative of the person, carrying out the building work]**

Figure 5: Examples of notices relating to waste water systems (Part H)

> **Cesspools**
> The foul drainage system from this property is served by a cesspool. The system should be emptied approximately every **[insert design emptying frequency]** by a licensed contractor and inspected fortnightly for overflow. The owner is legally responsible to ensure that the system does not cause pollution, a health hazard or a nuisance.
>
> **Reed bed treatment systems or other constructed wetland treatment systems**
> The foul drainage system from this building discharges to a **[insert type of primary treatment]** and a constructed wetland. The **[insert type of primary treatment]** requires **[insert details of maintenance of the primary treatment]**. The constructed wetland system requires **[insert details of maintenance of the constructed wetland]**.
>
> **Septic tanks**
> The foul drainage system from this property discharges to a septic tank and a **[insert type of secondary treatment]**. The tank requires monthly inspections of the outlet chamber or distribution box to observe that the effluent is free-flowing and clear. The septic tank requires emptying at least once every 12 months by a licensed contractor. The **[insert type of secondary treatment]** should be **[insert details of maintenance of secondary treatment]**. The owner is legally responsible to ensure that the system does not cause pollution, a health hazard or a nuisance.

8. Appendices

A. Extract from Approved Document L1

Summary guide to the use of this approved document

Routes to compliance for dwellings

STEP	TEST		ACTION
START	**Choose method of compliance**		
	Elemental method		Go to 1
	Target U-value method		Go to 5
	Carbon Index method		Go to 11
	Compliance by Elemental method		
1	Is the heating by gas or oil boiler, heat pump, community heating with CHP, biogas or biomass fuel?	No	Elemental Method not applicable – go to START and choose another method
		Yes	Continue
2	For gas or oil boilers, is the SEDBUK of proposed heating system ≥ SEDBUK from Table 2 in 1.7? [Note: for heat pump, CHP, biogas or biomass fuel, efficiency is not an issue, so continue]	No	Change heating system and go to 1
		Yes	Continue
3	Are all U-values of proposed dwelling ≤ the corresponding values from Table 1 in 1.3?	No	**FAIL** by Elemental Method – revise U-values and repeat 3 or go to START
		Yes	Continue
4	Is the area of windows, doors and roof windows ≤ 25% of total floor area?	No	**FAIL** by Elemental Method – reduce area of openings and repeat 4 or go to START
		Yes	**PASS** by Elemental Method and go to Additional checks
	Compliance by Target U-value method		
5			Calculate the target U-value (U_T) from equation (1) in 1.18
6	Is the heating by a system other than gas or oil boiler, heat pump, CHP, biogas or biomass fuel, or is it undecided?	Yes	Divide the target U-value (U_T) by 1.15 and go to 8
		No	Continue
7	For gas or oil boilers, is the proposed SEDBUK for the heating system equal to the corresponding SEDBUK from Table 2 in 1.7? [Note: for heat pump, CHP, Biogas or Biomass fuel, efficiency is not an issue, so continue]	Yes	Multiply the target U-value (U_T) by $$\frac{\text{Proposed SEDBUK}}{\text{SEDBUK from Table 2}}$$
		No	Continue
8	Is there a greater area of glazing facing South than is facing North?	Yes	Add: $0.04 \times \frac{A_S - A_N}{A_T}$ to the Target U-value (U_T)
		No	Continue

A. Extract from Approved Document L1 (continued)

Summary guide to the use of this approved document

9			Calculate the average U-value from $$\bar{U} = \frac{\sum AU}{\sum A}$$
10	Is $\bar{U} \leq U_T$ and is the U-value of each element ≤corresponding value from Table 3 in 1.29?	No	**FAIL** by Target U-value Method – revise and go to 5 or go to **START**
		Yes	**PASS** by Target U-value method and go to Additional checks

Compliance by Carbon Index method

11			Calculate the Carbon Index (CI) as defined in SAP 2001
12	Is the Carbon Index (CI) ≥8.0 and is the U-value of each element ≤corresponding value from Table 3 in 1.29?	No	**FAIL** by Carbon Index Method – revise and go to 11 or go to START
		Yes	**PASS** by Carbon Index method and go to Additional checks

Additional checks by builders

Limiting thermal bridging at junctions and around openings (see clauses 1.30 to 1.32)

Check that details comply with clauses 1.30 or that calculations show equivalence.

Limiting air leakage (see clauses 1.33 to 1.35)

Check that air leakage is limited according to clauses 1.34 or 1.35.

Space heating controls and HWS (see clauses 1.36 to 1.45)

Zone controls:	Check that zone controls comply with clauses 1.38 and 1.39.
Timing controls:	Check that timing controls comply with clause 1.40.
Boiler control interlocks:	Check that boiler control interlocks comply with clause 1.41.
Hot Water Storage:	Check that hot water storage complies with clauses 1.42 to 1.45.

Alternative approach for space heating and HWS systems (see clause 1.46)

Check that the space heating and hot water systems comply by adopting the relevant recommendations in Good Practice Guide 302 and that provision has been made to include zoning, timing and interlock features similar to those given in clauses 1.36 to 1.45.

Commissioning of heating and HWS systems (see clauses 1.47 to 1.49)

Inspect, commission and test systems OR check that the installation sub-contractor has certified, following commissioning, that the systems comply.

Operating and Maintenance instructions for heating and hot water systems (see clause 1.50)

Check that the building owner and/or occupier has been given information on the operation and maintenance of the heating and hot water systems.

Insulation of pipes and ducts (see clauses 1.51 and 1.52)

Check that reasonable provision has been made to insulate pipes and ducts, and that in unheated areas the central heating and hot water pipework has been insulated sufficiently to protect against freezing.

A. Extract from Approved Document L1 (continued)

Summary guide to the use of this approved document

Internal lighting (see clauses 1.53 to 1.55)

Check that reasonable provision has been made for occupiers to obtain the benefits of efficient lighting.

External lighting fixed to the building (see clause 1.56)

Check that reasonable provision has been made to enable effective control and/or use of efficient lamps.

Conservatories (see clauses 1.57 to 1.61)

When part of a new dwelling:

a) Check, where the conservatory is not separated from the rest of the dwelling, that the conservatory has been treated as an integral part of the dwelling.

b) Check, where the conservatory is separated from the rest of the dwelling and has a fixed heating installation, that the heating in the conservatory has its own separate temperature and on/off controls.

When attached to an existing dwelling:

Check, that where an opening is created or enlarged, provision has been made to limit the heat loss from the dwelling such that it is no worse than before the work was undertaken.

In addition:

Check, that with regard to the glazing, the safety requirements of Part N of the Building Regulations have been met.

© Crown copyright material is reproduced with the permission of the Controller of HMSO and the Queen's Printer for Scotland. An up-to-date version of this document is available at www.safety.odpm.gov.uk/bregs/brads.htm

B. Extract from Approved Document L2

Summary guide to the use of this approved document

Routes to compliance for non-domestic dwellings

STEP	TEST		ACTION
DESIGN			
	Choose method of compliance		
	Elemental		Go to 1
	Whole building method		Go to 25
	Carbon emissions calculation method		Go to 30
	Compliance by Elemental method		
1	Are all U-values ≤ the corresponding values from Table 1?	No	Revise U-values and repeat 1 or go to 3
		Yes	Continue
2	Are the areas of openings ≤ the corresponding values in Table 2?	Yes	Got to 4
		No	Reduce opening areas and repeat 2 or continue
3	Is the U-value ≤ to that of a notional building of the same size and shape as described in paragraphs 1.15-1.16 and taking into account the heating system efficiency as described in paragraph 1.32?	No	FAIL - revise design and go to 1 or go to START and test compliance by another route
4	Do all occupied spaces satisfy the solar overheating criteria in paragraph 1.20 et seq?	No	Adjust window areas or shading provisions
		Yes	Continue
5	Does any centralized heating plant as described in paragraph 1.25 meet the carbon intensity criteria of Table 5?	Yes	Go to 7
		No	Select different heating plant and repeat 5 or continue
6	Is the average U-value ≤ Uref = $\frac{\mathcal{E}_{ref}}{\mathcal{E}_{act}}$ From paragraph 1.32?	No	FAIL - revise design and go to 1 or go to START and test compliance by another route
		Yes	Continue
7	Do the heating system controls comply with paragraphs 1.33 and 1.34?	No	FAIL - revise controls and repeat 7 or go to START and test compliance by another route
		Yes	Continue
8	Does the HWS system and the associated controls comply with paragraphs 1.35 to 1.37?	No	FAIL - revise HWS system and controls and repeat 8 or go to START and test compliance by another route
		Yes	Continue
9	Does the insulation to pipes, ducts and vessels comply with paragraphs 1.38 to 1.40?	No	FAIL - revise insulation specification and repeat 9 or go to START and test compliance by another route
		Yes	Continue

B. Extract from Approved Document L2 (continued)

Summary guide to the use of this approved document

Routes to compliance for non-domestic dwellings cont.

STEP	TEST		ACTION
10	Is there general or display lighting serving more than 100 m²?	No Yes	Go to 19 Continue
11	Is the building an office, industrial or storage building?	No Yes	Go to 14 Continue
12	Is the average luminaire-lumens/circuit watt $\geq$ 40?	No Yes	Revise lighting design and repeat 12 or go to **START** and test compliance by another route Continue
13	Do the lighting controls comply with paragraphs 1.56 and 1.57?	Yes No	Go to 16 Revise the controls and repeat 13 or go to **START** and test compliance by another route
14	Is the average lamp plus ballast efficacy $\geq$ 50 lamp-lumens per circuit watt?	No Yes	Revise lighting design and repeat 14 or go to **START** and test compliance by another route Continue
15	Do the lighting controls meet the guidance in paragraph 1.58?	No Yes	Revise the controls and repeat 15 or go to **START** and test compliance by another route Continue
16	Is there any display lighting?	No Yes	Go to 19 Continue
17	Does any display lighting have an average lamp plus ballast efficacy $\geq$ 15 lamp-lumens per circuit watt?	No Yes	Revise display lighting and repeat 17 or go to **START** and test compliance by another route Continue
18	Do the display lighting controls meet the standards of paragraph 1.59?	No Yes	Revise display lighting controls and repeat 18 or go to **START** and test compliance by another route Continue
19	Does the building have any air conditioning or mechanical ventilation systems that serve more than 200 m² floor area?	No Yes	Go to 23 Continue
20	Is it an office building?	No Yes	Go to 22 Continue
21	Is the Carbon Performance Rating $\leq$ the values in Table 11?	No Yes	Revise ACMV design and repeat 21 or go to **START** and test compliance by another route Go to 23
22	Is the specific fan power $\leq$ the values given in paragraph 1.67?	No Yes	Revise design of mechanical ventilation system and repeat 22 or go to **START** and test compliance by another route Continue

B. Extract from Approved Document L2 (continued)

Summary guide to the use of this approved document

Routes to compliance for non-domestic dwellings cont.

STEP	TEST		ACTION
23	Are there any sun-spaces?	No	**PASS Elemental Method** and go to 34
		Yes	Continue
24	Do the sun-spaces meet the criteria of paragraphs 1.77 to 1.79?	No	Revise sun-space design and repeat 24 or go to **START** and test compliance by another route
		Yes	**PASS Elemental Method** and go to 34
Compliance by Whole Building method			
25	Select building type — Office:		Go to 26
	School:		Go to 28
	Hospital:		Go to 29
	Other:		Method not suited – go to **START** and test compliance by another route
26	Is the whole office CPR ≤ the relevant value in Table 12?	No	**FAIL** - revise design and repeat or go to **START** and test compliance by another route
		Yes	continue
27	Are the proposed building fabric performances no worse than those given in Table 3 and paragraphs 1.9–1.11 and 1.17–1.19 respectively?	No	Revise details and repeat 27 or go to **START** and test compliance by another route
		Yes	**PASS Whole Building Method** – go to 34
28	Does the school meet the requirements of DfEE Building bulletin 87?	No	**FAIL** – revise design and repeat 28 or go to **START** and test compliance by another route
		Yes	**PASS Whole Building Method** – go to 34
29	Does the hospital meet the requirements of NHS Estates guidance?	No	**FAIL** – revise design and repeat 29 or go to **START** and test compliance by another route
		Yes	**PASS Whole Building Method** – go to 34
Compliance by Carbon Emission Calculation method			
30	Does the notional building meet the standards in paragraph 1.75?	No	Revise notional design and repeat 30 or go to **START** and test compliance by another route
		Yes	Continue
31	Does the envelope of the proposed building meet the standards of paragraph 1.75(b)?	No	Revise proposed building envelope and repeat 31 or go to **START** and test compliance by another route
		Yes	Continue

B. Extract from Approved Document L2 (continued)

Summary guide to the use of this approved document

Routes to compliance for non-domestic dwellings cont.

STEP	TEST		ACTION
32	Has the calculation method been agreed as appropriate to the application (paragraph 1.76)?	No	**FAIL** - go to **START** and test compliance by another route
		Yes	Continue
33	Is the carbon emitted by the proposed building ≤ that emitted by the notional building?	No	**FAIL** - revise design and repeat 33 or go to **START** and test compliance by another route
		Yes	**PASS Carbon Emissions Calculation Method** go to 34
CONSTRUCTION			
34	Is the building control body reasonably convinced that the fabric insulation in the actual building is continuous (paragraph 2.1)?	No	**FAIL** - carry out remedial work and repeat 34
		Yes	Continue
35	Is the building control body reasonably convinced that the building is satisfactorily airtight (paragraph 2.2)?	No	Identify leaks, seal and re-test to meet standards of paragraph 2.4
		Yes	Continue
36	Has inspection and commissioning been completed satisfactorily (paragraphs 2.5 and 2.6)?	No	Complete commissioning and repeat 36
		Yes	**PASS Construction is satisfactory** - continue
PROVIDING INFORMATION			
37	Has the log-book been prepared (paragraphs 3.1 and 3.2)?	No	Prepare log-book and repeat 37
		Yes	Continue
38	Has a metering strategy been prepared and sufficient meters and sub-meters installed (paragraphs 3.3 et seq)?	No	Produce strategy / install meters and sub-meters and repeat 38
		Yes	**BUILDING COMPLIES**

© Crown copyright material is reproduced with the permission of the Controller of HMSO and the Queen's Printer for Scotland. An up-to-date version of this document is available at www.safety.odpm.gov.uk/bregs/brads.htm